What Others Say About Corpc

"Marrying your spiritual heart witl the most urgent imperatives of ot whole new vision of success. Shilpa has done a great job of inspiring you to do just that."

Nick Williams, founder of Heart at Work London, trustee Director of Alternatives and author of The Work We Were Born To Do.

"A thought provoking book that brings a new sense of direction for todays heavily worked and stressed executives."

Subhash Thakrar, Senior Partner, Blackstone Franks LLP, Board Director, London Chamber of Commerce and Industry Member, Bank of England Small Business Panel.

"Maximising corporate, financial and social success is the objective of every company today. Shilpa's experience in helping companies on this continuous journey is unique. This book can help CEOs, CFOs and other senior executives begin the journey via spiritual concepts."

Chandrakant Dhupelia, Chartered Accountant, formerly with one of the Big Four Accountancy Firms.

"In this insightful book, choc-full with spiritual wisdom, Shilpa has managed to provide a tool kit for living more successfully at work and always. I love the creative recipes and taster exercises that culminate in a path of self-discovery for all those seeking positive change on their journey. This book is a gift to anyone drowning in a stressful work dominated world who wants to integrate all aspects of their humanity even between 9 and 5pm."

Gill Fennings, Counselling For a Change, Therapist and Coach

Corporate Head, Spiritual Heart

Creating True Success and Fulfilment Without The Hang-Ups

Shilpa Unalkat

www.staflowpublishing.com

Staflow Publishing in 2006
Head & Heart Series

Corporate Head, Spiritual Heart

FIRST EDITION
Published by STAFLOW PUBLISHING in 2006

Head & Heart Series

ISBN 978-0-9552028-0-3

Edited by Sarah Best
Cover design by Danny Pinhas

A CIP Catalogue record for this book is available from the British Library.

The publisher offers special discounts for bulk order of this book. For information, please contact:

Staflow Publishing
PO Box 387
Stanmore
HA7 9BN
www.staflowpublishing.com

CONTENTS

ACKNOWLEDGMENTS

"Some people come into our lives
And move our soul to dance.
They awaken us to understanding
With the passing whisper
Of their wisdom...
They make our worlds more beautiful,
...leave footprints in our hearts,
and we are never, ever the same."

Anonymous

First and foremost, my heartfelt appreciation goes to **you**, the reader for selecting this book amongst the huge choice out there. I hope it provides you with an inspiring model for integrating spirituality into your daily routine and through practice, opens up a beautiful vista for a happier, abundant life. As you pass through each stage of your working years, achieving your goals and ambitions, remember your sense of humility, humour and humanity.

This book places an emphasis on you, the individual – on your personal growth. Through your awakening, your business is touched, the business touches your community, the community touches the nation and thereby the world is illuminated.

From the deepest place in my heart, I express my love and gratitude to my parents, Suresh and Chandrika Unalkat. Thank you for giving me the gift of life and honouring and respecting my dreams. Your belief in me has made all the difference.

To my sister, Anjali Raja, for being my best friend and for giving me strange looks across crowded rooms. Her comic genius makes me almost incontinent. To her calm husband Raj, for understanding the demands of true sisterhood.

To my gorgeous nephew, Shaan Raja, for teaching me about unconditional love and for opening my heart wider than I could ever imagine. You bring a sweetness in my life that soars way beyond words.

To my dearest friend and editor, Sarah Best. What this woman can do with a manuscript over lunch at Carluccio's is truly awe-inspiring. It has been an absolute pleasure working with you. I just felt it in my bones when we first met all those years ago in class, that we would be creating great things together.

To my uncle, Subhash Thakrar – your spiritual wisdom and presence speak volumes. Your encouragement has always been important to me.

To my soul brother, Vijay Mavani, who taught me what it means to have a generous and loving heart. Thank you Mr Maverick, for being the wind beneath my wings.

To my dearest friend, Arvind Devalia, for being a kindred spirit and without whose support this book would never have happened.

To Milan Zala – thank you for turning up in my life and making the cocktail magical. You have given me wise counsel and knighthood chivalry, complete with shining armour and a sword when needed.

To all my family and friends for being there during the brightest moments and darkest hours. For the joy and laughter you bring to my life.

The inspirational beautiful angels: Sukeshi Pabari, Rekha Thakrar, Usha Nair, Gita Pankhania, Gill Fennings, Sarla Hirani, Illa Gheewala Priya Lakhani, Ramilla Dhupelia, Lucie Feighan, Claire Raike, Tania Psathas, Vivienne Slater, Ruby Parmar, The Her Business Coaches, Dr.Mallika Punukollu, Kalindi Shukla, Marilyn Comrie, Shahzia Butt and Farah Hussain.

The strong honourable heroes: Mukesh Thakrar, Ajay Pabari, Chandrakant Dhupelia, Peter Kershaw, Sandeep Karia, Reg Athwal, Mehul Bakrania, Martin Boothe, Amechi Udo, Derek Browne and Maddy Orobator.

My favourite lecturer once told me that I would not choose my clients, they would choose me. He was right. I am grateful to all those incredible people from all walks of life, who have chosen me as their coach or attended my talks and workshops. All of you have enriched my life beyond my wildest dreams. I continue to find this process close to miraculous.

SHILPA UNALKAT
London, 2006

♥ ☺ ♥ ☺

The case studies herein are drawn from my coaching and hypnotherapy practice. The anonymity of my clients have been protected by altering names, places, occupations, details and other pertinent information. Although their identities have been fictionalised, the coaching benefits they have received are real.

ABOUT THE AUTHOR

Shilpa Unalkat, LL.B, DHP (MNRHP)

As the elder of two daughters, Shilpa grew up in a very loving, Hindu Gujarati family who arrived in the U.K, when she was a year old, just before Idi Amin's brutal Ugandan exodus in 1972. Shilpa was greatly influenced by her parents' strong work ethic, family unity and the well renowned entrepreneurial spirit of the East African Indian community.

What Shilpa received as gifts from her parents were an unquestionable sense of security and a deep appreciation for life and people. They wisely instilled in her the belief that with diligence, she could achieve whatever she wanted in her life. From childhood she was aware of the bridge between the inner and outer worlds through powerful ceremonial Hindu rituals, meditation and forms of yoga. The idea that the universe responds to us on many levels if we are ready to listen continues to be the ground of her psychological and spiritual way of being. It permeates and informs her style of working as a coach, trainer and therapist.

As a former city lawyer working in a magic circle law firm, Shilpa understands the pressures facing professionals in the corporate world. By teaching a combination of interpersonal skills, meditation practices and personal mastery techniques, she works to release her clients' desire for authenticity and personal power. The underlying philosophy is that the concept of total responsibility for one's life turns people's lives around.

Not only is Shilpa a masterful life coach with a busy practice, she is recognised as an exceptional mentor and frequently called upon by organisations as a motivational speaker. She is the founder and managing director of Staflow Limited, a personal & corporate development organisation, where she and her highly intuitive associates, collaborate with individuals who want to optimise their personal performances and create their lives in a more meaningful way. Clients discover what is deeply important to them and she nurtures their efforts toward what really matters most.

Shilpa's talks and workshops focus largely on developing personal power and effectiveness for individuals and organisations. Her workshops are fun, creative, and experiential with valuable, tailored content and are truly out of the ordinary! They help you think 'outside the box', making a profound difference to you and your organisation. For more information please e-mail her at shilpa@staflow.co.uk.

Shilpa is a full member of the International Coaching Federation and The National Register of Hypnotherapists & Psychotherapists.

Testimonials:

"Shilpa got me to think about the big question: How can I bring my business into an expanded sense of my spirituality? I applied this approach to every business situation and the results were remarkable. The answers led me to greater prosperity, both materially and spiritually. My new attitude makes me feel so good inside and leaves me with a clear conscience. Thank you so much Shilpa for helping me understand true freedom"

Akash, CEO, Import Export Business

"I instructed Shilpa at a time when I was under immense pressure. So much was happening in my business and I felt overwhelmed by what was expected from me as a leader. Shilpa was a real ally and gave me a supportive structure for step by step goal setting. She was also my inner ear, sensing and feeding back her impressions which turned out to be invaluable in terms of costs savings to the company. She helped me hone in my own coaching skills to get the best from my staff and to find out what their needs and issues were. I have learned so much about myself in the time we worked together."

Peter, Director, Software Company.

"Working with Shilpa is an upliftingly unique experience because of the quality with which she listens and the fullness of her commitment to her craft. There's a sense that she truly understands my quest for meaning in my life. She has the gift of an ancient wisdom that is refreshing in this modern world."

Clara, Intellectual Property Lawyer

"Having only had a few coaching sessions with Shilpa, I have already significantly improved my performance and attitude towards my role. I have been able to move past some tricky obstacles very quickly and addressed the real issues that I can actually do something about. I now have clarity about what works well (and what doesn't) and can concentrate on the areas that improve my results and the company's profit. Good coaching works and works quickly!"

Raj, Investment Banker.

"Shilpa is a truly dynamic and go-getting Business Coach and Corporate Trainer who brings years of experience into her consultancy. Her coaching has made it possible for me to take positive control of my life and business with a supportive and enlightening style that has boosted my self empowerment. I feel my whole life has now opened to so many more options than I could ever have dreamed of. Thank you."

Vivienne, Jewellery Designer.

INTRODUCTION

"This is the time of a great beginning. It is time to die to who we used to be and to become instead who we are capable of being. That is the gift that awaits us now: the chance to become who we really are."

Marianne Williamson, spiritual author and lecturer

Do you sometimes dread going to work because you feel overworked and unappreciated? Stressed and exhausted? Bored and frustrated? Have you ever noticed that you are so terrified of losing your job that your relationship with your company is not that different from that of a slave to a plantation owner? Most of us identify with at least one of the above during our working lives.

We know by browsing the job pages that good ones are hard to come by and that many people would love to take our place. There is no use whining about the burnout – we are meant to be grateful we're lucky enough to be gainfully employed. We must work harder and smarter and sort out our problems on our own. It is easy to feel isolated.

Do you sometimes feel as if you leave behind the 'real' you when you enter the workplace? Do you have two selves – a 'work' self and a 'non-work' self – that are so separate you can barely remember what one feels like when you are being the other?

Whether you are a managing director, social worker or secretary, work takes up a huge chunk of your life, so it is worth ensuring that it is as fulfilling as possible. This book will help you identify times and places when you are in the 'flow' or the 'zone' and teach you how to bring it into the workplace with you every day. This is the feeling of deep peace and connectivity we feel when we are enjoying living in the moment.

It is a state of total immersion in an activity, of working hard and enjoying it for the sheer joy of the work. It is a common experience of peak performers. Through my executive coaching practice I have helped countless people to bring this heightened awareness into their everyday lives. This book is a distillation of these experiences.

It is about the awakening of the soul at work and creating a culture that celebrates the unity of the intellect and the heart. For our work demands our heads *and* our hearts. They are partners, not adversaries. Our aim is to have the best of both worlds – the corporate head for its logical brilliance and the spiritual heart for its intuitive wisdom. Through this powerful union, we can create a balanced, fulfilling and caring work environment – an environment in which all have the chance to thrive.

We live in interesting times, some may say, materialistic, prove-yourself times. Through the media we often receive the message that attending to the yearnings of our soul is not going to buy us the high-flying lifestyle we should be striving for. And yet there are signs everywhere that a shift is happening. The time has come to be honest with ourselves and ask what is not really working for us anymore.

Visionary and humanitarian leaders are emerging in all fields of human endeavour, leading a not so quiet revolution, energised by the power of the soul. The business climate is changing. A new global reality is putting visionary leadership at a premium in the workplace. Interpersonal skills are highly prized, on a par with technical expertise. We want our leaders to connect and attune first with our feelings and personal ambitions as humans and then as workers. The astute amongst our leaders will not only recognise this shift in attitude, but also honour and embrace the inclusive spirit of this new approach.

Our corporate worlds have been dominated by an intellectual focus at the expense of the inner life and the wisdom of the heart. This disassociation from the heart causes us unhappiness and leaves us feeling powerless. There are countless Machiavellian-style business books seeking to teach us manipulative tactics for clinching success. We begin to see ourselves as warriors on a massive virtual reality crusade, all aiming for one thing – to push our way to the top of the corporate pyramid by knocking off the rest.

This book is *not* such an invitation. Besides, Machiavelli ended up a failure, and so did the princes who followed his advice. The back-stabbing politics he prescribed caused chaos in Italy for centuries.

Today's new consciousness is seeking to redress the balance, and it is no fleeting trend. It is our chance to make a real difference to a very important part of our lives. Could we be tired of inauthentic masks, mind games and greed? Revelations of corporate fraud and misdeed have led us to question fundamental human motives, turning us back to reaffirmation of basic values. Cynthia Cooper, the WorldCom whistle blower who informed on billions of dollars of financial fraud, says that her Christian faith gave her the courage to stand up against wrongdoing in her company.

On a personal level, we no longer want our lives to be measured in terms of how much we produce, but in the quality of our life experiences. We are more than our salary. This book is written from the premise that without spiritual fulfilment, material success is empty. And that spiritual growth is hindered when someone is chronically worried about their material security.

Daniel Goleman coined the phrase emotional intelligence when he noticed how some people seemed to get on and become successful without being particularly intellectually bright. Emotional Intelligence is the intelligence that understands moods, body language and cultivates self awareness and motivation. Danah Zohar formulated another concept beyond this idea – that of Spiritual Intelligence. This is a way of being that often chooses not to adapt and behave 'appropriately' and that uniquely steers away from mainstream. It is an intelligence that looks for vision and purpose and is transformative and creative. I am encouraging you to clear your mind of old and destructive thought patterns and discover new non-traditional ways of thinking! I am not alone in my quest. Spirituality is becoming a key theme within business academic research. Even some business schools are now offering MBA courses on spirituality in the workplace.

Common sense alone leads me to believe that 'spiritual' companies are better companies because of their higher ethics. They are also much more attractive to well-rounded employees who make it their responsibility to enhance their personal development, and ultimately their contribution to the growth of the business. There will be little or no divide between their home and work lives as the values are beautifully compatible and aligned.

Think about what you truly want from your workplace and then have the courage and wisdom to do something towards making this your new reality. Use the inspirational thoughts and quotes to uplift and encourage you to start bringing about a spiritual revolution at work. Aligning what we do, who we are and what we most value transforms our workplace into a playground where our soul is nurtured.

I am not suggesting you must do all the exercises at the end of the chapters (I am a realist!). Choose those that resonate with you. All I ask is that you pay attention to what moves in you when you do any exercise and listen for the call that dares you to take positive action. The exercises are there to help you discover some insights about yourself and your work environment and you may encounter some satisfying 'aha' moments. This shift in your awareness happens at a deeper level and not only will you have a solution to a puzzle, but you will recognise it as authentic truth. You may even be aware that something permanent has happened – a transformation has occurred.

This book has been written with an open heart. I invite you to read it with an open mind.

To the highest power that I am capable of reaching, I pray that You allow only truth to manifest here and may only the highest good result for all concerned.

PART ONE

REALISATION

CHAPTER ONE

The Corporate Condition: The Talented, Disillusioned Executive

"The feeling of being hurried is usually born of a vague fear that we are wasting our life. When we do not do the one thing we ought to do, we have no time for anything else - we are the busiest people in the world."

Eric Hoffer

On the surface she has the life she dreamed of as an ambitious young woman. She sailed through university and law school to become a successful corporate lawyer. At the age of 30 a lucrative partnership is within sight. It is hers for the taking if she can only work a little harder. She has a corner office, her own secretary, the respect of her peers, staff who look up to her.

She owns a large apartment in a desirable part of London. Her wardrobe is full of clothes that wouldn't look out of place on the pages of *Vogue* magazine. But sadly, this is a home she rarely spends time in other than to lay down exhausted at night. And she sometimes wishes these beautiful clothes were seen by people other than colleagues, clients and the hordes of anonymous people carefully avoiding eye contact with each other on the commute to and from work.

Every morning it's the same frantic routine. An alarm rips her from her heavy slumber while it's still dark outside. In her early twenties she took it in her stride, but as time went on she noticed her body was protesting more and more. The day came when she had no choice but to place the alarm clock at the other side of the room so that the snooze button was out of reach. The dash across the room to slap the clock into silence sets her heart racing and it doesn't stop until after she is back in bed that night – usually quite a while after.

In between, duty calls. She puts on a suit and a gladiator mentality, grabs her briefcase and makes a run for the tube station. Breakfast is a coffee and a croissant consumed with the same frantic urgency that characterises all her movements. By 8.00 am she is in work and there she will remain until that time in the evening, assuming it's not a particularly busy day. Twelve hours later, when she closes her computer down and picks up her briefcase, she desires nothing more than a warm bed, or bath, or embrace. But instead of following her instinct to hurry home, most nights she finds herself carried, as if on automatic pilot, to the smoky, crowded bar round the corner from the office.

It is an unspoken rule that anyone who wants to get ahead in the firm must spend at least three nights a week in here, back-slapping with 'the team'. Those who are really serious about success will be there four or five nights. A few glasses of Burgundy have the same effect as a valium pill. At least she can get to sleep on these nights. When she has not had her 'medication' she sometimes tosses and turns for hours, the minutiae of current law cases running through her head.

This young woman has success, status and money but what about peace of mind, joy and fulfilment? In the early days of her career she did not even notice she was sacrificing the latter three. After the carefree days of university she was hungry for a challenge, ready to throw herself into a career. But over time the buzz of the adrenalin rush has become deafening. Her mind too preoccupied to see her situation clearly, her body speaks to her in aches and pains and an almost constantly upset stomach.

She notices there are a few times when the physical discomfort goes away and her mind, too, is at ease. Hanging out with friends on a Saturday, preparing food and chatting away. On Thursday nights, sitting on a yoga mat chanting with other class members. On rare holidays or weekends away when walking through a majestic forest or horse riding on a Somerset beach. Anytime she watches her one-year old nephew greeting the world with wide-eyed amazement and playful love.

These are all windows into another dimension, and they open up a yearning within her. She tries to silence it by reminding herself that as nice as these experiences are, there is 'reality' to consider. There is work to be done, money to be earned, a mortgage to be paid, achievements to be notched up. Those special moments are very nice, but it's not as if we can feel peaceful, joyful and fulfilled all the time, she rationalises. Or can we?

That successful but unhappy young lawyer was me. And this book is the answer to my question.

SACRIFICING YOUR LIFE - FOR WHAT?

Tom Peters, who wrote the book, *In Search of Excellence*, said that excellence is a high-cost item and you must give up things to achieve it. He was referring mainly to professional and material excellence, and he said that what you must give up is "family vacations, Little League games, birthday dinners, weekends, lunch hours, gardening, reading, movies, and most other pastimes." In other words, the very things that make up our fondest memories; the activities that make life enjoyable, keep us out of the divorce courts and away from the doctor, and make life beautiful, balanced and graceful. It seems to suggest that all work and no play make you a valued employee.

My doctor once advised that one should never get so immersed in work that you give up other goals or responsibilities. No matter how satisfying our work, it cannot make our lives complete. You may miss out on the rich opportunities of a multi-faceted life. One of my clients, a banker, said that the best investment for him was taking six months out and spending quality time with his family.

Was what Peters called 'excellence' just another word for workaholism? The Japanese language has a word for 'death by overwork' – karoshi. You don't get a word like that in your language unless there are a few statistics to back it up. Workaholism, which broadly speaking is simply the compulsion towards busyness, has all the characteristics of an addiction. The worker becomes so preoccupied that it distorts their experience of time. They become compulsive and talk about work all the time, even if they bore the pants off everyone else. Often it has almost an 'anaesthetic' effect, covering painful issues in their personal life. You hear of people who lock themselves away in their offices and this cocoon comfort zone becomes a substitute for any sort of meaningful relationship. Their family are often quite upset by this and arguments flare up at home. When this becomes more serious, the person cannot function without this 'drug' and even hobbies or taking a holiday gives them withdrawal symptoms. Do you recognise these characteristics in yourself or anyone you know?

What sets workaholism apart from other addictions is that it is socially accepted. We don't bat an eyelid when someone says they are so busy with work they can't take a holiday this year – it seems almost impressive and indicates that the person is a hard working, productive member of society. Let's face it, it looks good and work is often used as an excuse to avoid certain situations or events. Hard workers do what is necessary to finish a project and then relax, whilst work addicts can't seem to stop checking and re-checking. As an employer you may think this is great and will increase productivity, but a workaholic environment creates burn-out quickly. Taken too far, so many health and psychological problems stem from what could be described as a narrow-minded, addictive mindset that dominates our work environment. The term 'type-A personality' was coined by heart specialists Meyer Friedman and Ray Rosenham to describe individuals who are competitive and hard driving. Not surprisingly they found that Type-A people are three times more likely to have a stroke or heart attack than Type-B people who take life more calmly.

It is no coincidence that the American Medical Association discovered some years back that the majority of heart attacks happen at around nine o'clock on Monday mornings. This undoubtedly has something to do with what most of us are doing around this time, which is going back to work. Or more precisely, going back to work we don't like, work that doesn't match our spiritual core, and work that can literally break your heart.

It is indicative of the society we live in, that the unhealthy drive and ambition exhibited by Type-A people is actually welcomed and encouraged in the corporate world. It can hardly then come as a surprise that many Type B people may feel pressurised to emulate these patterns of behaviour to be counted in for promotion. In my opinion the type-A personality is an unhealthy mental make-up. Underneath it there is always a voice, whether it is a whisper or shout, which tells us there is a better way. Over time this gets louder and louder and the end result could be a breakdown, burnout or even worse, a heart-attack.

AWAKENING YOUR SOUL AT WORK

Spend time with a two year old and you will soon hear the words "No!" and "Mine!" These are the cries of the ego which is just developing in the toddler. The ego tries to secure power by imposing its will. A central premise of the ancient Bhagavad-Gita is that a wise person performs work for the joy of the work itself, without attachment to results or rewards. In this way, one surmounts the ego and grows in wisdom and awareness. Yet how many of us can honestly say that we do this on a daily basis? Notice how when you give one hundred percent, you are happier and more enthusiastic.

Whenever I get a cab I often notice how some taxi drivers make my trip so pleasant with their cheerfulness, whilst others who are miserable make it a real pain and I just can't wait to get out! The ones who are friendly and relaxed are that way because they are giving a great service. When you are only thinking of the money and give only fifty percent, you suffer much more than your employer. He only loses a few pounds – you lose your self respect and a whole chunk of your life. Giving your best is the only way to enjoy your work.

Success does not have to involve negative tension. Do we really need to be struggling all the time? The ambitious tension can keep us in a state of contraction. It seems to give us energy, but doesn't really. It is akin to the immediate and short high we feel when we down an espresso shot. If you are involved in a conflict, ask yourself is it worth the struggle. Is it important? Does it have value? Will the outcome serve you or others? Often we are tempted to hold onto our position, especially if we have invested time and energy into it.

Imagine how the workplace would look if you softened your eyes. Maybe the gruff receptionist would seem kinder? It takes a surrendering and letting go for the softness to make its way into our hearts. We all know some people to whom this would be anathema, because it feels like defeat. Yet if we take the time to stop and realise that this is a form of mastery, of actually taking positive control over our response we can then begin to feel what a relief this approach is. It frees us and it frees others around us. A paradox is something that appears contradictory, and yet it is true. We 'control' by letting go – we 'win' by surrendering. We can even move forward by standing still. When we most want to force our will on someone that is when we should release. When we most want to have our own way that is when we should sacrifice. The irony is that by making these contradictory moves, we find what we are looking for.

One of my clients was a managing director in his mid-fifties. I'll call him Alan. Before coming to see me he was a high achiever who had climbed up the corporate ladder for over 30 years of career dedication and life sacrifice. He worked 12-hour days, travelled abroad at least two weeks out of every month, and had long been a near stranger to his wife and three children.

By the time he came to see me he had received a wake-up call. A routine medical check showed that his blood pressure was dangerously high. He was put on a very high dose of medication and warned that he needed to make some big changes in his lifestyle. At first he had protested, he told me, saying that it was the norm in his industry and there was nothing he could do about it. His doctor's response had been blunt: "And how many of your peers have died of a heart attack before the age of 60?"

This was the first time he had ever been forced to question the way he was living his life. It was the first time he had considered that he had choices about how to spend his time and energy; until then he had never stopped for long enough to reflect on the life decisions he was making, and whether there were better ones available to him.

We started off by getting clear about what his objectives in life were, so that we could then consider his options. He realized for the first time that he had been addicted to the adrenalin buzz his high-stress lifestyle brought him, but that it had never given him the depth of fulfilment he wanted. He also realised that following in the footsteps of the people he considered role models in the office was never going to bring him that fulfilment. After all, 33 years in, he was still waiting.

He took immediate action. Having chosen to take only about half his annual holiday allowance for as many years as he could remember, he announced that he was talking a four-week break. He and his wife spent a wonderful three weeks in the lakes and mountains of Italy, and the rest of the time was spent taking stock of his life.

He came back to me excited about the possibilities. He decided he was not ready to retire yet, but that he would start to prepare to do so within two to three years – much earlier than he had been planning. He was able to get transferred out of his demanding board-level job into a responsible yet much less stressful job in human resources. When I last saw him he had started evening classes in Italian, looking forward to another holiday and was excited about transitioning to flexible self-employment within a couple of years.

Unlike many unluckier people, Alan got his wake-up call in time. But why wait until you get that wake-up call? Much better to get your life into balance before you are presented with a make-or-break ultimatum. If you take an intelligent, happy frog and drop him into a pot of boiling water, what will the frog do? Jump out instantly! If you take the same frog and drop him into a pot of cold water, put the pot back on the stove and gradually heat up the pot, what then? He'll be merrily relaxing, thinking it's nice and warm here. Soon, you'll have a cooked frog. The moral of the story? Life happens gradually. Don't be fooled – be aware of what is really going on in your life.

SPIRITUALITY AT WORK

Spirituality, as I define it, has no religious reference. It is simply a way of expressing more humanity. For me, spirituality means being true to myself, living lightly upon the earth and being driven by a higher purpose. Spirituality has different meanings to different people. It has a lot to do with love, depth and reflection.

That which is spiritual:

- creates alignment of purpose and people
- comes from an inner knowing from the heart
- creates an inner peace or 'centeredness'
- is a *natural* desire to help others grow, learn, and succeed

What is spirituality at work? It is many things, big and small, simple and complex. It is bringing the integrity, consideration, compassion and honesty we demonstrate when we are at our best into the office with us every day. It is smiling at our colleagues and taking the time to get to know who they are *outside* of the organisation. It is feeling the creativity, flow and passion we feel when engaged in an activity we love every time we sit down to work, because our work *is* something we love. For those in positions of power it is taking care not to abuse that power. It is treating employees in a responsible, caring way, and making the organisations we run socially responsible in terms of how they impact the environment, serve the community or create social change.

REFLECT

Ask yourself what work means to you:

- Something that you begrudge because it takes too much of your time?
- A necessary evil that pays the mortgage and expenses?
- A challenge that excites you?
- A means of self-expression?

If you answered yes to the first two and no to the last two, your way of thinking about work needs to be transformed. Once you are answering yes to the last two, the blocks to fulfilment at work will melt away.

CHAPTER TWO

Let it 'Flow'

"I never did a day's work in my entire life. It was all fun."

Thomas Edison, inventor and businessman

It's your first day back at work after your summer holiday. You stare in disbelief at the pile of paperwork overflowing on your in-tray. You sit down and switch on your computer and are greeted with hundreds of e-mail messages awaiting your attention. You bury your face in your hands and for a moment are lost in memories – still fresh – of being by the ocean with the wind blowing in your hair.

Reluctantly you open your eyes and a post-it note stuck to your phone catches your attention: you need to call the firm's most difficult, demanding client – the one no-one wants to deal with. You listen to your voicemail: he has been trying to contact you and has left a series of increasingly impertinent messages. There is also a message from your manager insisting you 'touch base' with him by close of business. You let out a quiet sigh as thoughts of leaving early today vanish.

As your blood pressure rises and the migraine starts to kick in, you momentarily reflect on the inner tranquillity that pervaded your entire being during your relaxing family break. Remembering the playful laughter in the pool leaves you yearning to escape once again from the world of deals and results. What happened to the 'dedicated and enthusiastic' accolade in your appraisal? More to the point, what happened to that lovely state of inner peace and harmony you experienced on holiday?

Have you ever wondered why it is that you become so…so *human* when you are beside the sea walking hand in hand with your partner? You smile at travellers you meet on your journey and greet others as if they were souls you've known in another lifetime. Is this what the spiritual gurus refer to as the profound recognition of the spark of light in others? You interact fluidly with man and nature, appreciating and languishing in its beauty, so certain that there must be a master creator. You feel in awesome gratitude for the abundance of life. All is well within you. Appreciation comes easily. YOU ARE IN THE FLOW.

The good news is that it is possible to bring this state of 'flow' to work with you, every day. A silent inner knowing that this is something you would like to work towards is the first step.

TAPPING INTO THE FLOW AT WORK

To recap, the flow is a state of deep peace and connectivity. It is total immersion in an activity so that hours seem like minutes. It is working hard and enjoying it for the sheer joy of the work. Most importantly perhaps, it is being one hundred per cent in the present, with none of your mental energy focused on the past or the future. All of the above are common experiences of peak performers. When athletes talk about being 'in the zone' – and leaders in any sporting endeavour devote a lot of energy to being able to access this state at will – this is just another way of saying 'the flow.' Highly creative people tend to experience flow more often.

Think of the last time you experienced flow. Maybe you were relaxing on a beach, catching up with an old friend or engrossed in a great book. More interestingly, when was the last time you experienced 'flow' at work? How many times a day do you experience 'flow' while doing your job?

The first step is to pay close attention to what you are doing every day and notice how you feel emotionally doing different activities at work. I'm sure we are all likely to be happier at lunchtime! Some insights may come as a surprise, for example you may actually like the predictability of administration or working on your own. Some people may find they enjoy the interruption of calls to break their day up. We experience flow in our own unique way. Beethoven never heard his ninth symphony – he was stone deaf when he wrote it. Imagine feeling what it must have been like to have such a fire burning in the soul.

No doubt our surroundings affect our state of mind and we cannot all work by a lake or a mountain. We can however bring a little bit of nature into our offices. Maybe have a fish tank, pretty plants or crystals placed on tables and computers. Even getting rid of clutter can create a feeling of freedom and space.

It's an illusion to believe that we can leave parts of ourselves out of any environment or activity. Everything is personal. Why not be fully present? The personal evokes passion, creativity, and productivity. Every environment and every exchange offers an opportunity to deepen our spiritual work by putting it into practice.

Science has demonstrated that we don't end where our skin does. A field of energy extends beyond our body and affects everything around us. This energy can be negative and limited or positive and expansive. It is called *Chi* in Chinese and it is very powerful. Like attracts like so when we are at ease and present in our work, we radiate an expansive energy and we are treated in a far more positive way by others.

When you use your heart to plan your work, you start with a feeling. When you plan your work with your head, you start with a thought. A feeling resides inside your body, a thought resides in your head. Most of the time, like when you are reading this book, you have thoughts that turn into feelings, rather than a feeling that turns into a thought. When we use our feelings to make our plans, they turn out to be more powerful.

The way to know what your heart wants is to stop thinking about it. To discover your plan, stop thinking about it. Pursue something else. Spend free time doing something you truly love to do that you would not ordinarily do because you can't afford the time or the money to do it. It doesn't matter whether it's skiing, boating, painting, dreaming, hiking, running, or something else. For each of us it's different, but it does matter that you know what it is that does it for you.

I remember as a teenager, when I started having regular sitar lessons at home and struggling in my first six months to play a few chords on an unusual and relatively complicated instrument. After this initial learning curve, I began to understand the rhythms and nuances of Indian music and I started to give my fullest attention to playing with intensity. I felt a tremendous demand on my psychic energy but I was also totally focused, without the distracting thoughts of the initial months like 'God, I'm never going to get this right' or 'Damn, my finger is bleeding again and she still wants me to play another two raga's!' I was no longer self conscious and I felt a remarkable sense of oneness with the instrument and the music. Hours seemed to pass by and I was lost in another zone that made me feel quite powerful. It wasn't necessarily easy either – I did feel emotionally and physically stretched. A remarkable side benefit was how much more confident I became in all other aspects of my life.

Does this mean that every time we are in the flow we are happy? Mihaly Csikszentmihalyi (pronounced "Chick-sent-me high") in his highly researched book, *Finding Flow*, explains: "It is the full involvement of flow, rather than happiness, that makes for excellence in life. When we are in flow, we are not happy, because to experience happiness we must focus on our inner states, and that would take attention away from the task at hand. If a rock climber takes time out to feel happy while negotiating a difficult move, he might fall to the bottom of the mountain…Only after the task is completed do we have the leisure to look back on what has happened, and then we are flooded with gratitude for the excellence of that experience – then, in retrospect we are happy. But one can be happy without experiencing flow. We can be happy experiencing the passive pleasure of a rested body, a warm sunshine, the contentment of a serene relationship. These are also moments to treasure, but this kind of happiness is very vulnerable and dependent on favourable external circumstances. The happiness that follows flow is of our own making, and it leads to increasing complexity and growth in consciousness."

The truth is we spend little time truly loving what we do or doing what we love. Instead, we spend most of our time wishing that what we *are* doing could be more fulfilling. The reason for this is that we are mostly disconnected from our hearts, and we spend a lot of our time actively pursuing thoughts about what we *would* be doing if we were happy rather than experiencing what it means to be joyful in the moment.

The most productive business planning is not only thinking about end results, but experiencing the journey. It's not about getting things, it's about becoming more human. It's not about winning or losing, it's about taking the time to stop during your climb up the mountain to breathe deeply and savour the intensely sweet joy of the moment.

In his book, *The Power Of Now*, Eckhart Tolle beautifully describes how living in the moment, you will be so much more alive to all experiences, to all sights and sounds. When you are fully *here*, it is so bold. We become bored with life because we think we know it all – yet we don't know anything! The reason we don't know anything is because every moment is new – and how could you know something that is always new? Life becomes exciting if you make each moment something new to experience. Play with your keyboard, stroke your desk, notice the ink that flows from your pen onto the paper and enjoy the buzz in your office! This newness is where your life source comes from. Life is never old or finished; it is as new and as young as the moment you were born.

Connecting to your life source is about finding your joy and inner peace. This puts you into a truer, more meaningful relationship with yourself no matter what type of work you are doing.

Spirituality is listening to our inner guidance and should be our greatest resource when making decisions.

Building awareness of your emotional reality is extremely healthy, increases vitality, and reduces stress. To build awareness, learn to focus on your bodily sensations. For example, "I feel a knot in my stomach" could be a first step to acknowledging fear. Paying attention like this not only increases your awareness of your body and well-being, but can prevent unnecessary friction in the office. Once you can relax about your anxieties you can vocalise them in a calm manner which is assertive, not destructive.

I teach lunchtime meditation in the city and through reflective practice you open up a new consciousness and a deeper purpose in life. You find that your instinct and natural intuition is refined and you can see the truth amidst the chaos and then make a judgment with breathtaking clarity. I've come out of the closet and openly talk about peace and love in the boardroom. Most executives agree – peace of mind is a highly sought after commodity. I continue to be amazed at the wonderful changes in people who learned to really relax and go inside.

Remember the wisdom of Epicurus who teaches us about the three things human beings need to be happy. First is a sense of belonging in a community of friends. Second, freedom – the feeling that your life and choices are in your own hands. And third, a reflective life, which means having the time to ponder where you are going and what is important in life. We all need regular time in silence to connect with our inner voice.

EXERCISES

1. *Remove your head!*

This is one of the most intriguing meditations prescribed by the eastern guru Osho, also known as Bhagwan Shree Rajneesh. It has to be experienced to be appreciated. When you have a relatively stress-free afternoon in the office with no meetings arranged, just walk around in your room and imagine your head is no longer there, just your body. Continuously remember that the head is nowhere. You can even have a picture of your body without the head next to your desk. After a few minutes like this you will feel a weightlessness happening to you, such tremendous peace and silence, because it is the head that is the problem. If you can conceive yourself as headless – then you will be more and more centred in the heart.

2. *Take off your armour*

We all now know the story really well: living amongst aggressions and anxieties of our society, we have to protect ourselves, put the armour on each morning after the cereal. At the end of the day when we are home safe and sound in our cocoon of security, the armour can come off – theoretically!

Unfortunately sometimes it gets stuck and won't come off and we end up alone without relief and rest. Try the following for peeling off that tight-fitting armour:

At night before you sleep, take off your clothes and while taking them off, imagine that you are not only taking off your clothes, but your armour too – with all the strains of the day falling off. Actually do it. Take it off and have a good deep breath – then go to sleep as if unarmoured, with nothing on the body and no restriction.

When you wake up the next day, instead of putting on the armour when you put your suit on, this time imagine your suit is made of helium light – in whatever colour you feel like wearing on that morning. This is your protective light which is a gentle and friendly deterrent to predators. Imagine this light stays with you like a protective aura all day and notice how people react to you.

3. Tea Breaks

Buddhists invented tea to help them with their meditation. Tea is therefore a sacred substance for Buddhists – as well as for the English! Zen has transformed the most ordinary activity into meditation. Even if you do not have a Zen tea room in your office, you will be able to experience that deep reverence. Make it a ceremony; making tea or coffee...listening to the sound of the kettle, and then pouring the hot water, smelling the aroma of it, then tasting the drink and feeling peaceful and content. This moment you are alive! Feel thankful inside.

4. Be open handed

This is another unusual action that we would never usually think to perform. It is very simple but enormously rewarding, especially if you are a hard working business person.

Try placing your hands into the posture of a cup, like a receptacle. It is very meaningful, it helps you become receptive. It is one of the ancient Buddhist postures. Whenever you want to be open this will help. Sit silently and wait. Be a receptacle for abundance and joy, a receiving end. Just as you wait on the phone whilst you wait for your call to be answered. Just wait and within minutes you will notice a totally different energy surrounding you, filling your inside. There is a kind of softness and inner warmth and relief that results from such an unlikely act. Try doing it often in your hectic day and you will be surprised how much energy you will receive – it's all out there waiting for you after all.

5. Meeting of the hearts

We are so engrossed in our thoughts, worries and anxieties that very rarely do we meet someone with unassuming, non-judgmental eyes and with an open heart. This meeting is just a reflection of our tense minds and we are unable to connect with the other person. This simple method can help you immensely in all your relationships:

When you have a business meeting, settle within yourself, become silent. When your client or business contact arrives, feel a deep peace for them and welcome them with a smile. When you shake their hands, look into their eyes and connect on a deeper level. You will find a much more satisfactory connection based on honesty, trust and friendliness. Remember the Hindu tradition of greeting with a 'namaste' – it means 'I honour the soul in you'.

6. Work wise

A great part of our lives are spent at the office working, yet how many of us really enjoy working? We work as a duty and wait for the weekends and holidays to finally relax and take our masks off. Yet if we could bring a contented relaxation to our work, we will discover that work is actually not work, but is both pleasure and meditation!

This is a simple method that will bring a new quality of enjoyment into your work. Do this everyday if you can and soon you will see there is no difference between a business deal and playing with your children!

Whenever you feel in a bad mood and you feel a bit stressed out, before you start your day, just for five minutes breathe deeply. With every in breath, imagine breathing in positive light energy. With every strong exhalation, feel that you are releasing your dark mood out which is like a grey cloud floating away. It is simply a shift of emphasis, very simple and easy to do. You will start to do things more carefully and lovingly.

7. Experience you own space

Working in a large office can mean we are always surrounded by an intense people-filled environment. Tale a moment out of your day to experience an oasis of peace, by walking near some trees and feeling the earth beneath your feet. This will ground you. Some people also feel a calmness while washing their hands and allowing the flowing water to cleanse away any overwhelming emotions. Creating this space for yourself will help you energise for the challenges ahead.

CHAPTER THREE

Materialism and Maya: Weapons of Mass Delusion

'I am in a peculiar position. No one can give me anything. There is nothing I want that I cannot have. But I do not want the things money can buy. I want to live a life; to make the world a little better for having lived in it.'

Henry Ford

Why do you work? Think about it for a few minutes. At least part of your reason is likely to be financial. We all need money to sustain us. Yet if your ultimate goal is making money then you lose the fun of creativity and your motivation becomes one of getting rather than receiving. You compromise yourself and go for the hard sell and say things just to make a profit.

Have you ever felt like the proverbial rat on the treadmill funding mortgages, private education and the trappings of so-called success?
The precursors of material wealth – personal ability, education, rich relatives, the stock market – are not the true sources of stability. A portfolio that is spiritual in nature reveals infinite possibilities, surprising opportunities, and bountiful supply. This is the basis for

recognising our own real potential and discovering what is truly satisfying, dependable, and secure.

Tell you what: until you decide that other people's opinions will no longer dictate how you live your life; until you prefer the luxury of being the master of your own world; and until you conclude that life's too short to be enslaved by anything or anybody, least of all by smooth talking marketers, you will be susceptible to the largest epidemic since biblical times: *status anxiety*. In his satirical and humorous novel of the same title, author Alain de Botton wrote:

"The anxiety is provoked by, among other elements, recession, redundancy, promotions, retirement, conversations with others in the same industry, newspaper profiles of the prominent, and the greater success of friends. [...] Evidence of the inner drama is uncommon, limited usually to a preoccupied gaze, a brittle smile, or an over-extended pause after news of another's achievement."

There is something about the human psyche that feels the need for approval. Remember how gutted you felt when the rejection letter came in for that job you really wanted? Does it really matter whether that one interviewer sees you as worthy? Should you feel sorry for yourself because someone has said that the other candidate was more suitable? Let's remove the strain by suggesting we accept that 50% of the time we will not have approval and be happy when we have made 50% for the day – what a relief! Your life does not have to have total approval to be beautiful. No one who is being himself is going to be approved of all the time. Just *accept yourself.*

It is an unspoken secret most of us carry inside as we interact in an outside world where everything is pervaded by considerations of monetary worth. Consider the hypnotic power that is exerted over us by a sleek red Ferrari or a huge mansion overlooking the ocean with a tennis court and swimming pool.

What happens to us and inside us when we imagine or see these images in the media? The intensity of our emotions is raised by bonuses, designer labels and items of luxury. This buying into a lifestyle concept is exploited magnificently by marketing gurus to create glamour and illusion. It is like a drug and we become addicted over time. Are we buying into it? Look around you – what do you think?

We are too busy making money to spend time with loved ones. We may even fail to make it to our daughter's first violin concert.

Strangely, this is in an era where new technology is supposed to save time. What do we imagine that increased riches will really do for us? What is realistic and what is illusory in the power we attribute to wealth? Will it give us more power, more friends, make us become God?

What happens when we see redundancies or companies wiped out on the stock exchange? When we see our mortgage rates rising and unemployment and repossessions on the increase? I remember being disturbed for days having a nightmare in which I was a haggard old bag lady roaming the streets of London, completely destitute and hungry. Psychologists tell us that this is a very common dream. Such fears of scarcity creep in at times. Yet we have so much and not enough. Conflicts begin to fester inside of us.

A part of me has in moments of weakness, envied the wild, hedonistic lifestyle of the rich and famous. How wonderful would it be to have the freedom to do anything I wanted at any time? But how did that thought get inside of me? I don't remember letting it in. Do I really need so much and if so *why?* Looking at it rationally and truthfully, just how much of our time is swallowed up by unrealistic fantasies like winning the lottery and fears surrounding the issue of money? It is important to release any such feelings and focus on all that you *do* have. Bless the money you have and be open to receiving money from unexpected avenues.

It's great to be rich. Be ambitious - Be rich inside and out.

Money causes people more emotional problems than almost any other life issue. How many times have you heard that 'Money doesn't grow on trees', that 'Money is the root of all evil' or that anyone who is rich must, by definition, be either a crook or arrogant? Many people have negative associations about wealth and money that were gained subconsciously whilst growing up.

Money in itself is neither good nor bad – we attribute the element of impurity to it. It is the mind that is the source of greed and money is one of the places where it expresses itself. It is our attachment to money that is the issue. Money is a symbolic medium of exchange among humanity, to represent accumulated creative energy. It symbolises energy flow. To see it as a sacred trust to be used for the good of all humanity is the highest view of it.

You can't take your money with you when you die! We have all heard that saying. From a higher perspective, we can ultimately possess nothing on the material level – although it might possess us because we are too attached to it or worried about it! Nothing truly belongs to us – it's all on loan from the universe during this lifetime. When you understand that we take nothing material with us you can begin to see how travelling lightly is so liberating.

We can be good custodians of what we have been blessed with. We can keep our resource channels clear and flowing and harmonised with the universal laws. When we care for and improve what has been entrusted to us, and release to others things that we no longer use, we see a new inflow of abundance. An attitude of gratitude brings us an inner peace that is far more valuable than monetary possessions.

We have seen examples in the media of how the self absorbed life focused on personal indulgence leads to disillusionment and finally, despair. Those who create a set of higher values around having money – values such as generosity and integrity, discover they are living life at its deepest level.

Check inside: Are you compensating for something?

If you think you could not live without your impressive job title or sports car keep this in mind at all times: it is not the job title or the car that your soul yearns for, but the *feelings* these things give you. That can be a range of things, from security and comfort to excitement and challenge. There is, in my opinion, one thing underlying it all: a false perception of lack. In my experience as a practicing psychotherapist, I've come to realise that most clients I have seen have some kind of self-esteem issue at the root of their problems. People simply don't feel they are *enough* – good enough, smart enough, successful enough, attractive enough – and that's why they need external 'props'.

So much of our energy goes into 'looking good' in front of others and we tend to pursue whatever it is we think will secure us the approval and status we hunger for. The plastic surgery is often just elastoplast over a deep and, it seems, universal psychological wound. It speaks of a deep insecurity, a feeling that you are not adequate and need validation to be on this earth. We may find it helpful instead to make a conscious decision to find less costly, not to mention more direct, routes to fulfilment.

Responsibility can put you on the map.

Robert Kiyosaki is a man who added to the wealth he had created through property and other business deals by writing about his two dads – one rich, one poor. *(Rich Dad, Poor Dad: What The Rich Teach*

Their Kids About Money That The Poor And Middle Class Do Not!). Back in the early 1970's he was getting rich on the back of other people's misery and poverty. His lifestyle made him a magnet for beautiful women, fast cars and invitations to the hippest parties. Yet he found out that although his rich dad had taught him how to make money, he had failed to find deep personal meaning and fulfilment through living purposefully.

"When Buckminster Fuller asked me what my purpose in life was, I honestly didn't know. What I did realise was that I couldn't continue getting rich from Korean factories populated with child labour", says Kiyosaki. "I hate poverty, and what ultimately caused me to quit rock and roll merchandising was when I saw those young kids squatting with their knees up to their ears in order to increase the square footage so I could make more products and get more money." He now educates children about finances and it costs him around $2 million a year to make his *'Cashflow For Kids'* game available to any recognised educational institution in the world.

The big question on all our lips is how to achieve financial security with some spiritual component. More of us are questioning what we were put on this earth to do. Is it really to play golf all day or to watch reality TV most evenings? "Money does not make you, it reveals you," Kiyosaki concludes. "We're not here to make money, we're here to solve the world's problems and make life better for everyone. That purpose goes on, even when you have money. Likewise, a key ingredient for making money is being of service to humanity. That's the ninety degree approach that will fill the hole in your soul."

On a deeper level, some people evolve much better in poverty. They will move when in extremity, but do nothing when things are pleasant. You will always be presented with what is needed for your growth. If poverty brings up fears for you – wonderful. You can use this for your spiritual unfoldment. There is nothing wrong with being poor, except in feeling poor. If you have learned the deep soul lesson about the fear of poverty and have completed the cycle, without you doing anything, prosperity will move in.

PUTTING PASSION FIRST

A client of mine – I'll call her Milly – was a senior executive at a leading PR firm, but her passion lay elsewhere. Now in her forties, she had loved animals since she was a child, and was an active supporter and campaigner for several animal welfare organisations. A year or so earlier, she had begun devoting her PR services for free to one charity, and found that this work inspired and motivated her like nothing she had ever done before. In the meantime, her day job had become less and less fulfilling with long hours, too much travel and a work environment she disliked intensely.

Worse still, her firm did PR for several companies which exploited animals, such as a fashion house which used real fur and a pharmaceutical company which used animals for experiments. When she was told to manage an account for the former, she realised that she could no longer stay at this company as the work she was being asked to do was so at odds with her ethics and values. I sensed in Milly a compassionate philanthropist who wanted to make a difference in the world.

Milly was a real goal setter, understanding that without them, the future chooses us. We started by looking at her Wheel of Life. This helped her identify goals in eight key areas: physical environment, health, money, personal growth, recreation, relationships, work and family. Under each of the headings she rated her level of satisfaction on a scale of 0 (totally unsatisfied) to 10 (totally satisfied). There were some interesting surprises for her! We looked at what she needed to do and was willing to do to increase the lower ratings.

Next, we researched what her options were. Although she was open to other paths, she was so excited about the possibility of a career in the animal welfare field that we concentrated on this first. She already knew that she would be taking a huge salary cut, but I got her to research specifically what she could expect to earn in this sector, and whether that was realistic for her. The result: she would be earning less than a quarter of what she earned today, with only modest and gradual salary increases and no expectation of ever reaching her current level nor even close to it.

However, as Milly was single with no children, her mortgage was paid off and she had a healthy portfolio of savings and investments, she was willing to take the cut. In fact, by this time, she told me, she was so passionate that she would work in this field for free! Being paid any amount, however small, seemed like a bonus to her. She would have to cut her spending a great deal, but that didn't matter, she told me, as much of her spending was tied up with the lifestyle her job imposed on her: designer clothes, salon treatments, socialising with colleagues at the best clubs and restaurants in town, and so on.

The next step was for Milly to look at the charities she could approach and research the positions available. She decided that although she'd enjoyed her time with the organisation she'd been doing volunteer PR work for, it wasn't the one for her as it was in a busy part of London and she wanted to move out of the city. She homed in on a charity in Sussex that was looking for a press officer. A month later she was offered the job, and she hasn't looked back since. She has exchanged her flat in London for a house by the sea, and on our last coaching call she told me that she feels much richer than she has ever felt in her life. The change I saw Milly experience in a short time was dramatic, yet the first seeds of it had been sown many, many years earlier.

Why do some people give up lucrative jobs for a riskier endeavour? They do it because the latter fires their souls, and opens the way for unrealised potential. As they say, purpose and passion – discover one and you find the other and often they have nothing to do with the money.

A report prepared by investment bank Dresdner Kleinwort Wasserstein in November 2005 provides a mass of evidence that shows that people who focus on more materialistic goals are less happy and healthy than those who prioritise relationships or personal growth. Spending on experiences rather than items makes people happier, the report found. Therefore, money is best channelled into activities with friends and family like concerts and holidays, rather than being used to amass possessions like a fast car, bigger house or a designer bag. The report also found that: "Not only are people who pursue materialistic goals setting themselves up for a generally unfulfilling experience, but they are considerably more prone to mental anguish and problems as well."

In the words of Lao Tzu:

Chase after money and security

And your heart will never unclench

Care about people's approval

And you will be their prisoner

Do your work, then step back

The only path to serenity

BRINGING MORE OF OURSELVES INTO THE GAME

People often ask me how it is possible to make a sales process of transferring a product or service to another in exchange for money into a meaningful transaction involving the heart. I remind them that the important thing to remember is that with every project or sale, you are making a connection with someone else. Without that connection there would be no sale. The essence of spirituality is being in the present. The essence of a successful connection is your ability to be in the present.

This means being able to tune into the other person's needs, feelings and thoughts. From a spiritual perspective every connection with another person is an opportunity to be of service. When we provide a service that truly benefits others, without creating harm anywhere, then a fair and equitable profit for the work done is in order. Profit allows this service or good to continue to be provided to others.

The famous spiritual text *A Course In Miracles* puts it beautifully: "When you meet anyone, remember it is a holy encounter. As you see him, you will see yourself. As you treat him, you will treat yourself. Never forget this, for in him, you will find or lose yourself"

US chat show host Oprah Winfrey once wrote in *Oprah* magazine: "Use me, God. Show me how to take who I am, who I want to be, and what I can do, and use it for a purpose greater than myself." Can you imagine having a life goal that is bigger than yourself, to have a cause beyond personal wealth and pleasure? *A cause that will touch the lives of others and bring meaning to your work?* Many successful leaders in business, such as Jeffrey Swartz of Timberland Shoes, have demonstrated the power of living their values. Swartz pays his employees to volunteer in the community.

REFLECT

What is of ultimate value? What is there that is not a means to something? What do you pursue for its own sake alone? For me, its things like creativity, love, beauty and connection with others. These are the treasures just waiting to be grabbed that give life so much meaning and satisfaction. When the shallowness of materialism becomes self-evident, these things remain and continue to deliver their promise.

Ask yourself the following questions:

- Will the world be better for my having been here?
- Do I need to leave my deepest values at the workplace door?
- What will last when my work is over?
- What could I start doing straight away to bring more meaning to my life? Teach swimming to disabled kids? Grow bonsai trees?
- If I continue to live my life this way, will I be able to look back – in one year, five years, twenty years – and feel a sense of honour and integrity about what I have created?
- When I get up in the morning and come face-to-face with myself, do I like who I've become? Am I a living model of the very things I say are important in my life?
- Am I the example I would want my children to follow?

CHAPTER FOUR

The Corporate Mask

"The challenge for business leaders in the twenty-first century is to assume the mantle of spiritual elder for their cultures, so that life doesn't become trivial and grey for all the people who spend most of their life at work."

Jim Channon

There was a time when companies, even big ones, were like families and employees were cared for like children. Loyalty and competence were enough to get you through and you could even expect a job for life. The employer-employee relationship was one based on loyalty and mutual respect. But those days are now long gone, booted into touch by years of restructuring and heavy redundancies.

With the IT revolution, many of us are excited by the rapid developments, but at the same time feel uncertain and vulnerable. This is where seeking strength in spirituality and human connection can play a very beneficial part.

The greatest spiritual challenge arises when we are part of an organization which has a dysfunctional culture. Employees at all levels have the responsibility to influence this reality and make it healthy. Spirituality at work requires that we work to change the culture so that sound business practices are followed. When confronted with the challenge of shaping corporate culture, it is important to follow the advice of Reinhold Niebuhr, seeking the "serenity to accept the things we cannot change, the courage to change those that we can, and the wisdom to know the difference."

How do you get clear about the cultural values in your organisation? Attitudes reveal values – so begin by noticing the prevailing attitudes around you in the office. Often the cultural values of our workplace influence us in subtle ways. Becoming more aware of these influences can free us to choose when we will support these values and when we will offer an alternative.

WHAT IS YOUR ORGANISATION'S ATTITUDE TO TIME?

In *The Age of Paradox*, Charles Handy states that modern industry has turned time into a commodity. Our culture is almost obsessed with time: finding enough of it, making the most of it, saving more of it. But even with all the attention we give it, we're rarely truly mindful of how we spend it.

- Are you expected to put in long hours and pay your dues to earn your partnership or directorship? If you don't, are you considered unprofessional, uncooperative and unwilling to renounce your self interest for the greater good of the organisation? Do you risk losing promotion, pay rises or even perhaps your very job?
- Do you have to stay at your desk after normal working hours? Are client needs paramount in terms of unrestricted availability and tight deadlines?
- Do you sometimes stay at work even though you have nothing to do just because you want to be seen to be 'putting in the hours'? In some companies there in an unspoken rule that says if you leave before a certain time you are not a dedicated employee.

A client of mine who is a financial journalist once confided in me about the above. When she started her traineeship as an enthusiastic graduate she planned to get her work done between 9am and 5:30, the hours on her contract. Evenings, as far as she was concerned, were for socialising, going to the gym or the movies or just relaxing and unwinding at home. But she soon realised this wasn't to be and it was nothing to do with the workload.

On her first day, she threw herself into the work and was way ahead of schedule for meeting all of the first week's deadlines when she turned off her computer at the end of the day. She had noticed that her new colleagues did not seem that motivated and that their desks were not exactly hives of activity. She was the only person to skip out of the office at 5:30 pm; no one else made the slightest move. The following day was the same. On the Wednesday of her first week she cancelled the plans she had made for that night and stayed put, curious to see what time the others would leave.

At seven o'clock everyone was still there. She had no work that needed doing, so spent her time surreptitiously observing her colleagues. One was leafing through a tabloid newspaper. Others were engaged in emailing or talking to friends. She noticed that others were also nervously looking around checking what everyone else was doing. When she had been there a couple of weeks the features editor who sat behind her confided that it was not the 'done thing' to leave before 7.00 pm, and if you were really serious you'd stay much later. Anyone who wanted to please the managers had better put in the hours, regardless of whether they had anything to put *into* those hours. Soon, she found herself working less effectively during the day because there was no incentive to get work done quickly.

More and more firms now give employees realistic workloads and encourage them to get out in the world and develop other parts of themselves once their work is done. Such firms breed a much more efficient, stable, well-rounded workforce. The word 'clock-watcher' has made its way into the workplace vernacular. In my opinion it should not be a derogatory term, but a compliment!

Which is the more effective employee? Someone who is efficient and motivated during the working day, and leads a happy and fulfilling life? Or is it the stressed, miserable employee who lacks both the efficiency and the well-roundedness of the 'clock-watchers'? If you have a life, you will be watching the clock to make sure you don't spend too much of it at work. It's as simple as that!

Whilst working in New York as a corporate lawyer I was required to carry a pager around with me after working hours in case I was needed urgently to attend to some legal work for this very important multi-national client. I was enjoying dinner on a Saturday night with friends and had to leave my delicious cappuccino cheesecake halfway, to rush back to the office, only to find that the matter could have waited until Monday morning!

Later on, back in London, I worked for a firm that had rooms with beds on the top floor! The underlying message: "You don't need to go home! If you're not sleeping you should be here working. Why waste time commuting?" This may be an extreme example, but many firms have spoken or unspoken policies that encourage employees to become one-dimensional corporate robots.

WHAT IS YOUR ORGANISATION'S ATTITUDE TO ETHICS?

- Is acting with integrity encouraged or is it a *lack* of ethics that gets rewarded by your firm?
- Could you challenge the status quo where you feel that others are not acting with integrity?
- Do the values of your workplace or profession run counter to your own values or to the values of your spiritual tradition?
- Are their websites/marketing literature consistent?

Joe Tye, author of the book, *Staying On Top: When The World's Upside Down,* offers this advice for staying true to your ethics at work: "In a way that does not impose your own religious beliefs upon others, commit yourself to being an example of someone who lives according to high moral values and deep spiritual faith."

As a young lawyer working on the pensions fraud scandal in the early 1990s, I was stunned each time I saw my managing partner routinely double the amount our client owed and quote that number on the invoice. This, of course, would ultimately be at the expense of the poor pensioners who had already lost so much. When I gingerly challenged the partner, he went red in the face; not out of embarrassment, but out of anger. "It's a complex case," he snapped.

"That is reflected in the £300 an hour fee," I wanted to reply. Yet I was all too aware how risky such boldness would be.

How many of us allow a huge gap to exist between the values of our private lives and the values of the workplace? Community, contribution, generosity, love and sincerity may be important to us at home, but in the workplace we are often rewarded for independence, competition and acquisition. This is ideal breeding ground for jealousy and toxic emotions.

If your spiritual values are important to your mental well-being, then at some point you will have to take a stand. In today's climate you can afford to be a visible example of your own spiritual values. You must decide whether you can live with any gulf between your ethics and those of your organisation. In the end, integrity always pays off and if it does not happen at your current firm you will soon outgrow that firm and move on to somewhere more in line with your ethics.

WHAT IS YOUR ORGANISATION'S ATTITUDE TO SPACE?

Your work environment and the space you have around you are vital to your well-being – this allows you breathing space and the freedom to get on with things. Companies like Intel Corp and Coca-Cola Co provide space for workplace Bible classes as well as for other religious groups. At the Body Shop, cleaners can use the board rooms for meetings.

Are you crammed in the office or do you have a comfortable work environment?

- Do you have plants, air-conditioning and water tanks for your comfort?
- Is there a cafeteria, and if so is it a spacious, friendly, bright place people like to congregate during work breaks – or not?
- Are there any relaxation facilities such as quiet rooms, a meditation room, a gym?

WHAT IS YOUR ORGANISATION'S ATTITUDE TO COMMUNICATION?

Communication is the tool that allows people to work together. In our society, our learning process is based on communicating with teachers and parents (usually, by learning how to *avoid* punishment). When we go out into the world, most of us have not learned how to communicate with our peers for the purpose of achieving something beneficial for all of us. We constantly try to win the favour of the 'parent' or 'teacher' or 'adult' – usually a management figure. We try not to get punished.

This behaviour leads to subterfuge among employees: trying to work out how to beat the system, gain extra favours, say the popular thing or to keep our views to ourselves rather than 'rock the boat'. Our true voice is lost. Just imagine instead what it would be like if we were rewarded for being more or even totally truthful in the workplace – honest self-expression would flourish.

Ask yourself:

- Can you discuss anything, including your feelings about work and non-work issues with management?
- Is there a forum for two-way discussion between employees and management?
- Do management have an open-door policy; i.e. are they easily approachable? Or are they shut away on another floor of the building, and unreceptive to staff approaching *them?*

As an executive coach, I work with many high performers who for one reason or another go through some real lows at work. One thing that they often say is how little their organisation really cares about them. They complain that the relationship at work is purely an economic one and if only they were more nurtured, that would release so much more of their inner potential which is just waiting for expression. If we feel that our firm values and respects us, it counts for a lot when deciding whether or not we stay in our jobs. This is only possible if there is an open channel of communication between management and employees.

WHAT IS YOUR ORGANISATION'S ATTITUDE TO TRUTH?

When truth is compromised, trust and confidence begin to break down. It becomes acceptable for staff to tell lies in order to step up the ladder of success. Substance starts to matter less than subterfuge; reality less than perception.

Common examples of lies include:

- "Tell the customer what he wants to hear. All that matters is the sale."
- "Your job is secure." (followed by the person being made redundant).
- "You *will* get positive results in this research project. We need the grant to be renewed."
- "That was not sexual harassment. It was just a bloke being a bloke. Ignore him."
- Do different people give consistent answers to the same question? Are they looking for honest answers or trying to second guess what you want to hear? Second guessing suggests that the habit of honesty has faded.

WHAT IS YOUR ORGANISATION'S ATTITUDE TO FAIRNESS?

We all want to compete on a level playing field, but do we all ascribe to equal opportunity regardless of race, sex, age, religion, or disability in the real world? The answer is obviously not often enough. Discrimination can happen via the informal systems of the old boy's network, or the unseen glass ceiling. Abuse in the form of discrimination is hidden but very real. It flies in the face of the myth that all of us are created with equal opportunity. Just imagine how loyal and productive people would be to a system that treated them fairly.

Ever come across any of these: discrimination, overwork, harassment, systematic humiliation, withholding of resources, financial manipulation, hidden agendas and smothering big brother policies? What do they have in common? They all have their human cost. What sort of human cost? Stress, headaches, nervous breakdowns, heart-attacks – all have been linked to working environments that breed fear and hostility. There is also the effect on relationships, families and self esteem.

Ask yourself:

- Do women have to work twice as hard as men to get the same promotional opportunities?
- Do management often exclude minorities such as non-whites and gays?
- Does your age matter when it comes to the issue of promotion?

WHAT IS YOUR ORGANISATION'S ATTITUDE TO CREATIVITY?

Creativity includes the use of imagination, laughter and freedom to enhance productivity. Creativity is fun and when people enjoy what they do, they work much harder. It includes conscious efforts to see things differently, to break out of habits and to let go of out-dated beliefs to find new ways of thinking, doing and being. People are naturally creative but when they are forced to crush their creativity, the repressed energy force turns to destructive release as their inherent humanity needs to express itself.

Ask yourself:

- Do you get credit for your good ideas?
- Are you encouraged to suggest changes for improvement?
- Are you allowed to experiment and make mistakes, or does fear of getting things wrong stifle creativity?

GREAT CORPORATE COMMUNITIES

A lot of effort goes into making companies look inviting, successful, and fun. Many companies now provide a wide array of work-life balance programs. They place great verbal emphasis on healthy employees. Gyms, health clubs, and childcare provision all suggest that companies will keep your best interests at heart.

Yet the question I am most often asked is: How can I tell whether a particular company will be a great place to work? Somehow the buildings and the policies don't seem to answer that question. Most often, I'm asked the question by women who are constantly trying to read between the lines to find out whether a company is female friendly.

We've learned the hard way that what you see is not always what you get. It seems to get harder and harder to get a true picture of a company before you join. Great places to work are not about skyscrapers, mahogany boardrooms, and corporate jets; they are about great *ccommunities.*

Here are some aspects that employees who are going for interviews should look out for – and that employers who want to hire loyal, competent and discerning staff need to pay attention to:

- Does the interviewee get a chance to meet people at different levels of the organisation and ask questions? A culture of openess and trust is evident when things are done openly, for instance, doors are generally open, there are open areas and glass panels where meetings can be seen.
- Is there a distinct hierarchy? For instance, do only the junior staff get the coffee ? My boss often used to ask the team if he could get us a drink when he popped out for a bite to eat. We felt really good that he had no qualms about this at all.
- Are the diversity policies fair? As an interviewee, can you see people like yourself in the top levels of management? If you are female, black, disabled, or gay and don't see anyone like that on the board or at least at higher managerial levels, you would be entitled to be pretty sceptical about diversity policies.
- Employees are keen to find out the take up rate of sabbaticals and maternity/paternity/stress leave policies. Work-life balance is increasingly important to both the sexes. Is there an unspoken, hidden price attached to taking leave? Even younger employees who do not have children now are still concerned about what happens when they do. What happens when elderly parents need us?
- Do people openly talk about outside hobbies or holidays? Does the sparkle in their eyes remain when the conversation reverts to work?
- Who are the heroes and villains of the office. Those who are admired will show us *what* is admired.

In looking at corporate cultures, perhaps the greatest single indicator of all is retention: How long do people stay with the company? In companies with fast staff turnover, no one builds strong relationships – what's the point if your colleagues are going to leave next year?

Many companies are finding the most effective way to bring spiritual values into the workplace is to clarify the company's vision and mission, and to align it with a higher purpose and deeper commitment to service to both customers and community.

Companies are moving away from blanket solutions that might not suit every worker – such as granting specific religious days off – to more subtle accommodations like prayer rooms and use of company computer networks for faith groups.

Recent research by Tim Osborn-Jones, Henley Management College's expert in organisational behaviour, proved that the economic part of a manager's benefits package does not carry as much weight as the non-financial elements. A group of 476 Henley alumni were questioned about their relationship with their employers. Of the replies, 11% were couched in what Osborn-Jones describes as transactional terms, while a compelling 52% came down in favour of a relationship contract. "It's complex, but my evidence is that most managers are still looking for a relationship with their employers. They want a more effective relationship with issues such as aspiration, equity and community remaining important. My argument is that for those who have the talent and can make a choice this is what counts."

In today's environments, it is not just money that keeps people attached to their place of work. More and more, companies are being forced to offer workplace conditions and contexts that support life overall: not just on the job, but in the area of personal well being and quality of life. Employees are becoming much better informed about what ties them down and what doesn't.

Corporate and personal growth comes through responsible change. Your organisation may have it's problems, but instead of justifying continuing outdated, old patterns, blaming others for the way it is, you need to take charge. Assess your workplace, see that there is a need for change and start that process. *Any choice you have made, you can change.* Accepting the responsibility of making your own choices in your work will give you the power to move in your world with confidence and strength.

REFLECT

- What three words would you use to describe the principle values of your workplace or profession?
- Are the values actually practiced differently than the 'stated values' or mission statement of your organisation?
- How has your workplace or profession shaped you since you began your work?
- Have you noticed that things once very important to you are less so now?
- How have you shaped, or could you shape, your workplace culture?
- Does your workplace encourage, tolerate or discourage diverse and individual perspectives? How? What could be improved?

CHAPTER FIVE

Team Play

"Individual commitment to a group effort – that is what makes a team work, a company work, a society work, a civilization work."

Vince Lombardi

During one of the Special Olympics in the USA, nine finalists with disabilities were competing for a gold medal. Half way round the track, one of them fell. He tried so hard to get up, only to fall again. He tried again without success. Finally he just lay there and began to sob. One by one the other contestants heard his sobbing and stopped running. They headed back and helped him up. All the contestants then held hands, walked down the track and crossed the finish line together. The crowd were thrilled – they couldn't believe their eyes. They rose and gave a 15-minute standing ovation.

When I read this, I was so moved. This was one of our finest moments; humanity at its best. We are all capable of such great heights. Deep down it feels right when we step in to help out a fellow human in need. This is not an intellectual sort of knowing. This is the way of the heart. When we feel deeply, we are dealing with the soul. It is as if our soul is in heaven at that moment.

Have you noticed how the desperation for success sometimes brings out the baser primitive survival instinct? They don't call it the urban jungle for nothing! Our hearts sink and our souls constrict when we continuously endure the ruthlessness of a cut throat and competitive work culture.

We become less interested in achieving higher standards in our work and more keen to protect our positions through deceptive ploys and defensive tactical moves. At such times our vision is clouded by fear and suspicion. We cannot even come alive at home as this state of mind we have in our jobs has robbed us of so much energy that there is nothing left to give. Our spouse and children see us exhausted and at times we cannot cope and our tempers run short at the smallest request from them.

A self-preservation work culture has led us to construct protective, artificial shields in front of our hearts. Fear turns our creative, fertile minds into a wasteland and transforms normally reasonable people into bullies. You only need to read a few employment law cases to appreciate the unhappy outcomes.

Remember the scene in the movie Star Wars where Luke Skywalker confronts the dark side of The Force in a tunnel, and it turns out to be a reflection of himself? We all have a darker side which is most likely to emerge in a tough environment.

It is hardly surprising that so many people have issues in this area. In school, we learn 'team' work by competing with each other and competing with other teams. We aren't usually taught the kind of true team work that involves everyone emerging as a winner and an equal. No, it's about finishing first, coming out on top, defeating the opponent. Unless we are incredibly aware and conscientious, we carry this conditioning into our workplaces.

Roger Salient, CEO of Plug Power, one of the first electric fuel cell companies says that work at his organisation "[…] is not *your* job or *my* job. It's *our* job. And that's how people become enlisted when we are working together. It's what happens when you think of yourself having no boundaries, when you think of yourself as working in a field of connection and consciousness"

When a group of people are committed to a common purpose, are given responsibility, and at the same time feel supported and trusted, then, and only then, will they tap their deepest potential. Emotional energy, not mental energy, is the true motivator of the human spirit.

AGGRESSIVE COMPETITION

I used to believe that my so-called killer instinct helped me become successful. As a young, litigation lawyer, I took great pride when my managing partner referred to me as a 'Rotweiller in court' to our opponents. So I was taken aback when I learned that in many recent studies, the results suggest the *less* competitive one feels, the more one will succeed. In his enlightening book, *No contest: The Case Against Competition*, Alfie Kohn found compelling evidence that competition is toxic, not only to the job, but also to the soul. He shows us how competition causes the following:

- Poisons relationships
- Makes us suspicious, hostile and envious
- Destroys our self esteem
- Creates anxiety and the need for approval
- Is inefficient
- Undermines genuine love of learning by focusing on external gain
- Kills curiosity.

He argues that competition is aggression. So what is the alternative?

- Co-operation and partnership.
- An atmosphere of co-creation. We can work together to come up with fresh ideas. No one has to do it alone – and what a relief that can be!

When we are working in a competitive environment we can become blocked emotionally. Have you noticed that when you feel deeply, either the excitement of joy, or the sadness of sorrow, you immediately become more open and alive? Even if we are moved just a bit, we have transcended our normal, routine physical concerns. When we are under pressure, our hearts and minds are constricted and we can't see beyond our physical needs and desires. Our sensitivity to spiritual arousal is blocked, our capacity for higher awareness is limited and we focus on mundane things.

In business terms, a harmonious economic interaction is called the 'meeting of minds' or 'goodwill' and is the basis of all contracts. We sense that we can't be completely dominated by the mundane forces of corporate life. We want our intellectual perceptions to come around to the perspective of the heart, so what better place to start than with our fellow colleagues?

More and more great leaders of our day find that the best way to work is to draw on the strength of others, to build teams and to develop synergy. After all, it gets lonely achieving goals on your own. To bring a team together and see the dream realised together brings community to success and vice-versa. How about we forget about ladders to the top? Think instead of a group journey on a boat with everyone supporting each other. And if someone accidentally falls overboard there will always be someone ready to jump in to save him. This is the 'You win, I win' attitude. Individual success should not mean the failure of others.

Sincerity is the essence of the spiritual heart. But manipulation is the cloak of a clouded mind that is driven by ego. This includes slyness, scheming and under-handed attacks on colleagues. We can learn a lot from small children – their behaviour has a total absence of artificiality. A child's very soul is expressed in each of his activities. He is transparent. His soul shines in everything he does. Imagine what it would be like if we retained that state into adulthood. How would you feel if you could be like that at work? What stops you?

A 'spiritual relationship' with others is not necessarily one in which we are smiling saints all the time. We are not here to audition one another, put others on trial or use them to gratify our needs. We are not here to fix, change or belittle another person. **We are here to support each other and to grow from this experience.** It is easy to find fault with your fellow workers and get irritated when they do not see things your way. Sometimes this tension builds up leading to frosty encounters at the coffee machine.

Also, life mirrors what is going on inside you. If you feel challenged by others all the time, decide instead to focus on behaviours that show the best of human nature. Commit to seeing every little thing in your workplace as a potentially spiritually enlightening experience.

THE POWER OF COMPASSIONATE PRAYER

Most of us find ourselves addressing a Higher Power in times of great stress and trauma. Even confirmed atheists may find themselves on their knees with hands clasped together when things are really bad and they see no other option. What really happens if we are honest is a form of begging with a few desperate promises.

Though they are often answered, there are much more powerful ways of praying. How many of us take the time to offer a prayer of thanks and gratitude every time things are going well? When the universe sends you something you like, acknowledging that invites more of the same into your life.

Praying out of gratitude is very powerful, but most powerful of all is praying on behalf of others. How many of us routinely pray for others, especially others who are not in our immediate circle of family and close friends? Not only does such prayer benefit you and those you are praying for in subtle ways through healing vibrations. It also reminds you that we are all connected. If you do this regularly, you will find it much harder to fall prey to the dog-eat-dog, cut-throat mentality. The highest form and finest energy we can work with is *unconditional love.*

- One female client who is a director of a major P.R company has the practice of praying for each member of her staff. She has about 100 employees. She feels this is an outgrowth of her own spirituality.
- Another Hindu client has a statue of Lord Ganesh in his office who is the remover of any obstacles. He does a short prayer before he begins any important work or contracts.
- A senior partner of a well known accountancy firm always does a silent prayer before he starts a meeting and asks that the outcome is beneficial to all attending.
- I often use my commute time for my daily meditation and prayers - to pray for my clients' well-being and happiness. This is my spiritual gift to others.

LAUGHTER – THE UNIVERSAL PICK-ME-UP

Many of us are very serious at work. Often the first thing to go in the workplace is the very thing that helps us keep things in perspective: our sense of humour! What is it about humour that makes life easier to live? What is the connection between humour and health, vitality and the ability to go the extra mile? Healthy energy is energy that is moving like when we are happy, laughing and even tolerant as opposed to being stuck, unhappy or rigid.

Work is a place where we have been taught to rely on our heads – our intellects. We constantly think things through and reason things out. Often, in order for us to do this successfully, we have to put aside what's going on in our bodies. We ignore what we're feeling and what our instincts are telling us. We push down and push away the information that the body carries, so that we can make 'reasonable', 'logical' and 'rational' choices based on our analysis. Yet it is now well established that self awareness and recognising a feeling as it happens, is the cornerstone of emotional intelligence.

Humour happens in your body when you are relaxed. When that laughter rises from your stomach through your mouth and brings with it the sound that brings relief around the boardroom table, think what is actually happening? Think of the last time you laughed until you cried. Remember how your heart felt. Remember how your muscles tightened and caused your body posture to shift and your presence to take on a whole new shape? Laughter is increasingly being recognised as a powerful form of therapy and laughter centres are appearing all over the globe.

However, it is worth paying attention to the kind of humour that pervades your workplace. Are things easy and light? Or is your humour dark, often dismissive of someone or something? Is the humour barbed and cynical? Do you shroud nasty comments aimed to hurt others with the words: "can't you take a joke?!"

In order for light-hearted humour to be present in the workplace, there has to be a sense of safety and acceptance: that it's okay to say what's on your mind and to say things that fly in the face of the status quo. It's not about being a threat, but about creating and contributing and making a difference. Tolerance is a fluid energy which brings about goodwill. Be conscious of ways that you can keep this energy moving in your body as well as in the office.

If you want to create work environments that support and sustain life, start by making friends with what's going on inside of you. Notice when your guts tighten and your lips form a tight, straight line. Notice when you are holding your breath.

Start to have fun at work with your peers. Go ahead – share a joke and a laugh! People who enjoy their life work harder, make more money and have more confidence in themselves. They have more friends and are far healthier than those people who worry constantly. Celebrations spontaneously arise when people feel connected. You see that in offices where the group buy a birthday gift and call a special meeting to wish a team member happy birthday or good luck in a professional exam.

Greet each day with a sense of awe and an expectation of wonderful things. Before too long, you'll be seeing magic and joy, instead of stress and heartache. Smile when you see someone, welcome a new employee, and compliment a colleague on their work. Whether you are at work, at home or on holiday, your **attitude** about your life defines how your life unfolds. It is *how* you do your work and connect with people that really matters. From a spiritual perspective, a successful life is one in which you radiate more good than bad vibrations or energy. Make a choice today to live the fullest life possible - filled with friends and enjoyable work. The world will then be a better place for all of us. To hold the world in our hands, we must give ourselves to it.

REFLECT

Starting today, see the world in a different light. Be creative. Visualise difficult situations as if they are a cartoon with funny characters. See the humour in things. Put a smile on your face, learn to see the beauty all around and take a deep breath. Instead of criticising someone, count to 10 when frustrated, and take a walk instead of clenching your teeth. Think about how our light can shine brightly together, creating even greater light.

A blessing is an expression of thanks or a prayer. I see it as a transfer of energy which helps others to fulfil their potential. It is an act of service. A blessing should come straight from your heart, with sincerity and we can do this by deliberately going into the most loving mood of which we are capable. This may seem really hard sometimes, but we are all equipped to do it if we try! You can bless a difficult situation, even if the person involved may not be receptive to your efforts. There may be something that touches your heart and evokes compassion. For me it is babies and so if someone upsets me I imagine them as a vulnerable baby or a child full of innocence, before I am able to do a heartfelt blessing. Blessing the situation helps you to understand and discover the good and the lessons in the experience. It allows us to move with grace and humility and rise above what seems negative.

A blessing is a natural act that we can all do and is not just restricted to priests or gurus. The most common way is to use your hands as a conduit for this benevolent energy, but if you feel shy or embarrassed then do a silent blessing in your mind. Don't forget to switch on a huge inner smile and feel the lovely, vibrant change in your body.

When you are at work, silently offer the person on your left and right an appropriate short blessing. Imagine your silent words creating a healing light energy around them which connects to your own energy level and strengthens your working relationship with them. Breathe gratitude and acceptance into the moment – make it real and see the difference.

CHAPTER SIX

Serve To Lead

"The leader shows that style is no substitute for substance...that creating an impression is not more potent than acting from one's centre."

Lao Tzu (Chinese philosopher, 6th Century B.C.)

Imagine the Dalai Lama in a smart bright orange cotton suit with a black dotted tie with his fingers touching in a triangle shape, his elbows leaning on the mahogany table in the boardroom. Forget the macho images of a leader – the real strength of a leader is the ability to inspire others to greatness.

The word 'leadership' is an old English word that actually means to go first. The consciousness of the leader has a significant impact on the consciousness of the organisation.

If we are going to change the system we need courageous individuals to risk liberating their minds from the mechanistic thinking of the 'command and control' ways of running a company. "You can't transform a group structure without having the leadership go through some sort of transformation," says Richard Barrett, author of *Liberating the Corporate Soul.*

Vision means seeing beyond the obvious – seeing the unseen. Where does vision come from? For some, it is an inborn trait. They can always see things beyond the perception of others. Visionaries see a vision of what can be, of possibilities beyond the status quo. They then follow their vision in spite of obstacles and non-believers. I believe we can all learn to be visionaries. Anyone can learn to broaden their perspective, to question the obvious, to reach beyond where they are, to follow a dream. The only requirement is a strong desire to want to learn, coupled with a strong desire to grow and expand where you are.

A visionary may dream wonderful visions of the future and articulate them with great clarity. A visionary is good with words. A visionary leader is good with actions as well as words, and so can manifest his vision. More than words are needed for a vision to take form in today's world. It requires heartfelt commitment and enrolling the participation of others. Commitment is essential; as Goethe said: "Until one is committed there is always hesitancy, the chance to draw back, always ineffectiveness."

A visionary leader can stand strong and secure in the presence of others who also feel strong about themselves. They are not shaken, threatened or jealous of other people's power. In fact they honour and welcome the strengths of others. Visionary leadership is based on a balanced expression of the spiritual, mental, emotional and physical parts of ourselves.

I have witnessed these amazing qualities in one of my clients, who is a director of a multi-national food company. She lives by her commitment to be truthful. She prefers to be straight-forward. Sometimes she has failed to deliver on time, but she tells the customers exactly how it is and they still remain loyal. Lies or games are of no interest to her, but she's not easy to fool. She is experienced in the ways of the world and can size up a situation very quickly. I believe she is a great leader – she understands human mistakes and weaknesses but does not condemn them. She knows when cow manure is being thrown around and finds constructive ways to handle internal conflicts. She has a steady and even temperament that adds an element of stability to any situation. One thing for sure is that she likes a good laugh and is refreshing in her spirit and lack of pretence. She encourages her staff in their goals and aspirations and lends support when needed. One of her staff members said to me that: "She really cares for us sincerely – we know this because she gives her time generously and we find her approachable".

DOING WELL BY DOING GOOD

Spiritual values that could be widely embraced in business include integrity, honesty, accountability, loyalty, quality, co-operation, intuition, trust, respect, equality, and service. A commitment to values is an outstanding characteristic of all visionary leaders who embody a sense of personal integrity, and radiate energy, vitality and confidence. More self-aware and reflective than others, such visionary leaders follow and lead from an inner conviction. Mahatma Gandhi is a prime example of someone committed to his core values, as he freed India by appealing to the moral conscience of Britain and using 'satyagraha' or non-violent action to usurp the immorality of the British Empire.

In 1989, two professors of the Stanford Business School, Dr James Collins and Dr Jerry Porras, analysed over 100 successful executives with whom they worked. Their conclusion reflected that the ingredients common to each were a sense of *purpose, mission and vision.* They had a sense of destiny that gave them a compelling future to aspire to.

This is perhaps a good time to write down your own core principles and values. This exercise may be a wonderful moment of revelation and truth for you. You will learn a lot about yourself, particularly what drives you. Take a few minutes now to think about this. The key is to reflect deeply and write out your personal mission statement. For it to be effective you must read it regularly. Why is this so important? As James Callaghan, former Prime Minister of Britain stated: "In my judgment, a leader should have a core philosophy and belief against which he can judge the important issues as they arise. Unless he has that bedrock to fall back on, the unexpected storms that blow up will toss him about like a cork. Without such a foundation, a leader may be able to survive, but he won't be a leader in the sense that I use the term"

You will find that identifying your core principles and values will give you a sense of purpose and meaning. To give you an example, here is my personal value statement:

To inspire and empower people to live their highest vision in a context of joy and spiritual growth.

By writing it down and reading it every day, I have developed a commitment to it. So this means I will always know how I will act in any given situation. The result of such a deep commitment to one's values is *personal power*. It is an invigorating force that fills you up and lends you the courage to be great.

This power comes not from the core values alone, but from the strength of one's commitment to them. It takes personal dedication and personal reminders. Since we are in such a busy world, we are often so task-focused that we forget our inner core values that drive us. The challenge is to constantly keep reaching within ourselves, pulling out our values and staying true to them. Unless people do that, their spirituality will not take root. It's not really magic – it's about transformation using post-it notes and pocket books if that is what it takes!

On a deeper level, true power always comes from the Divine. It passes through us and then flows out into the world. When we understand this relationship, we are blessed because this flow brings with it a tremendous feeling of expansion and fulfilment. We feel we can accomplish anything. Problems develop when we forget we are not the source of this power, only its conduit. Power should not intoxicate us to obscure our good sense and we must use it wisely.

This list outlines some commonly held values. Which ones are important to you?

Variety	Creativity	Challenge
Freedom	Reputation	Being the best
Power	Status	Independence
Intellect	Security	Respect
Spirituality	Intimacy	Family bonds
Integrity	Commitment	Trust

As an extension of the above exercise, now think about aligning all your actions and behaviour to your core values. The secret to a successful career is realising that it is not separate from the rest of your life, but an extension of your inner self.

Once when Mahatma Gandhi was speaking in England, he held a group of people spellbound for several hours without any preparation and in a relatively uncomfortable environment. The crowds were enthralled by what this remarkable man had to say. Reporters were amazed that he was able to speak so convincingly without any notes. His secretary, Mahadev Desai explained: "What Gandhi thinks, he feels; what he says, and what he does are all the same. He does not need notes". He was all lined up, and at one with himself and his core values.

How lined up are you with your core values?

Once we line up our deep commitment to our core values with our actions, we have **integrity**. We will be at one with ourselves. Imagine what a powerful way of living that would create for us.

When I walked away from a profession I'd served for ten years, I didn't think I had anything in common with people who take the bull by the horn and are true to themselves. But in fact, I actually did. It was a scary and very isolating walk off a cliff called 'security'. That was the only way I could be honest with myself. I was comfortably successful and didn't have to leave. Most days I liked the paycheque that funded my bellini nights out, my ever increasing fondness for Jimmy Choo's, and having my very own P.A. who booked my spa weekends for me. Yet there was something missing and things just began to get at me. Complacency set in and I felt I needed more of a challenge. I didn't feel I was running away from anything, it was more like moving towards a new fulfilling life. I needed to test my mettle as a soloist building my own consultancy and branding. This thought excited me like no other and just stayed with me day and night.

I wanted to experience the emotions that Michelangelo once did as he created his sculptures from his imagination. I wanted to feel my work with that kind of rare, magical intensity. Looking back I have no regrets. The journey has been awesome as I have had the opportunity to find the most challenging, creative and karmic work since then. To me, success is also knowing that I have on a deeper level, energetically helped humankind and the earth. When you belong nowhere you begin to question who exactly you are when you leave. Quite unexpectedly, my commitment to my core values carried me forward to the inner work of personal and spiritual growth. Each of us at some point in our lives takes a stand alone. But the moment we do, we find kindred spirits who have also taken those brave steps.

True character is not being worried about being popular – it's about doing what is right, not what is necessarily convenient. When you put effort into aligning your actions with your core values this results in **trust.** People **sense** when you are acting out of deeper values and you will find people are more willing to follow your ideas, suggestions and contributions to your organisation. Without it they feel something isn't quite right and may sense manipulation and only follow you grudgingly, if at all.

Notice how great visionaries stir up energy in others – they are not running around all over the place. Their personal power is like an invisible force around them that inspires others to get things done. This aura makes them attractive and like a magnet they draw the right people and circumstances that lead to success.

If we change our values to suit the occasion or our current mood, it is like having no anchor and we are at risk of drowning. However, if we self-correct our behaviours to match our core values, this usually *increases trust.* Visionary leaders can apologise and rectify their behaviour as soon as they realise that their values and behaviour are out of sync. They do this quickly – they do not dwell on it or bend their values to fit in with impulsive actions or thoughtless behaviours.

Those leaders that we admire and look up to have all 'failed' at some point in their lives, and they continue to do so. They too have doubts to overcome, demons to face and disappointments to make peace with. People look to leaders to make decisions, and they can't always be warm and fuzzy. They stay clear and focused in their vision especially when they are under pressure or perceived attack. They are following higher principles and that makes them a force to be reckoned with.

In the words of Dee Groberg, founding vice president of the International Covey Leadership Center: "It takes courage to stay true to what you believe and to self-correct when you are wrong. Because it is difficult, it offers an opportunity for greatness." Such leaders also offer hope and guidance to those who are struggling with their own actions and trying to line up their actions with what they really believe. When we treat others with respect and allow them to self-correct and grow, we give them value. Imagine feeling validated and valued. What sort of environment would that cultivate?

PULLING THE PEOPLE LEVER

Influence is about empowerment – and not just your empowerment. Many people feel disempowered and disengaged at work because they lack influence. Remember the last time you heard a salesperson say: "I can't do anything about that – it's not part of my job. You need to write to our head office." The servant leader would say "I totally understand how you feel. What you need to do is to take the complaint to X. Here is her direct number. I'm going to call her now to brief her." How different would that make you feel?

Anyone can be influential, not just people in positions of power. You might help someone feel more confident so they can handle a complex matter or teach them a new skill. *A candle loses nothing by lighting another candle.*

Become aware of the many possibilities you have for influencing others and that will help you become more aware of your own value. Influence is about offering others something that they will be glad to receive – whether that is practical help, emotional support or constructive criticism. Influence in this sense is a valuable currency increasing the value of the organisation as a whole.

IMPOSTOR SYNDROME

In all walks of life, there are leaders who believe they do not deserve their success. It has become so prevalent that psychologists have invented a new term for it: 'neurotic imposture'. Writing in a 2005 article in *The Guardian,* Insead professor of leadership Manfred Kets de Vries said: "To some extent, of course, we are all impostors. Displaying a facade is part and parcel of the human condition. But neurotic impostors feel more fraudulent and alone than other people do. Because they view themselves as charlatans, their success is worse than meaningless: it is a burden. 'Bluffing' their way through life (as they see it), they are haunted by the constant fear of exposure. With every success, they think: 'I was lucky this time, but will my luck hold? When will people discover that I'm not up to the job?' "

A neurotic impostor is a perfectionist who sets impossible goals; in other words, who sets him or herself up for failure. For many, the root of the problem is the fear that success will cost them too dearly; often, specifically, the fear that family, friends and others will continue to like them much better if they remain 'small'. The mindset can lead to self-destructive behaviour which, ironically, often brings about the very failure that keeps such people awake at night.

Not everyone who carries around this heavy psychological burden is a leader, but in my personal experience leaders are especially prone to it. One of the most dangerous side effects of neurotic imposture is its possible effects on decision making. Leaders who feel like impostors are afraid to trust their own judgment. Their overly cautious kind of leadership can easily spread across a corporate culture and cast a shadow over the whole company.

A person's strengths are also her weaknesses and neurotic imposture is the flip side of leadership; in fact, it is a rare leader who does not suffer from it to some extent, at some time during their careers. Therefore, it is important for leaders to be on the lookout for it in themselves and their subordinates. Encourage a culture where open, honest feedback – including constructive criticism – is freely given and warmly welcomed. Always be sure to give praise where it's due, and make sure your staff know that making mistakes (and learning from them!) is part of a successful corporate culture.

SERVANT LEADERS

Ken Blanchard, Bill Hybels and Phil Hodges brilliantly describe the term 'servant leader' in *Leadership by the Book: Tools To Transform Your Workplace*. They maintain that leaders who are servants first will assume leadership only if they see it as the best way they can serve. They are 'called' to lead rather than driven, because they naturally want to be helpful. They use their talents and abilities for the greater good of the organisation.

They love feedback from those that they are serving because that will help them serve better. They welcome accountability and want to know if they are helpful. They are not threatened by differing opinions. They want to listen – but it is not about pleasing everyone! The authors use Jesus Christ as a true model and symbol of the servant leader as he came to earth to serve and *not* to be served. Unlike the kings of the past, he did not rally his people to fight in bloody battles and die for him. He died for his people: the ultimate sacrifice for the greater good.

This is a model radically different from the prevailing reality in the corporate world. It is based on the development of character and sound intentions rather than behaviour. It is not service driven by ego, nor by the 'status syndrome' where we are always trying to get others to serve us. The servant leader asks 'what can I do for *you*?' People do not normally associate business with generosity and kindness, because business is seen to be only a tool to make money.

The biggest debilitating compulsion in the corporate world today is to automatically consider every question from the point of view of 'What's in it for me?' The paramount aim of servant leaders is the interests of those they lead. Personal power, money or recognition is never the focus. They are willing to share power with the purpose of equipping others to become more autonomous, capable and free. Servant leaders get great personal satisfaction from watching others grow and develop their skills.

Servant leaders value and demonstrate democracy and inclusiveness, by listening and creating empowering relationships. They only accept as much authority as people are willing to give them. The work gets done by inspiring workers with vision and by example, rather than dominating them. This approach creates 'power with' rather than 'power over' – a co-operative blend of leadership and empowered equality.

Servant leaders educate rather than simply direct. They inspire responsibility rather than create dependency and they assume that people already have the potential wisdom and creativity within them and their task is to draw this out. Servant leaders help others to develop self-confidence and a sense of self-worth. As the ancient Chinese sage Lao Tzu said "Leadership is best when the people say, 'We have done this ourselves!'"

RECAP

To engage the heart at work is:

1. to see people as people, not as employees.
2. to assume an intention of good will on their part.
3. to recognise a job well done, not just with money but also with a genuine appreciation. The 'you get your thanks in your pay cheque' attitude produces cynicism and resentment in workers.

4. it is to remember that people are creative and capable. It is to believe in them, not just the numbers.

To engage the soul at work is to realise listening to people, responding to them, is not a waste of time. Next time a colleague comes to see you, try making a point of looking up and pushing your chair back from your desk: the message you give is that you have time for them and give them your full attention. They will feel at ease so they can tell you what they want to say. What use is communication without honesty?

This perspective affects the quality of the interactions in the organisation, creating positive rather than negative feedback loops. That is, creating trust and commitment, rather than suspicion and disconnection. Can you see how this can transform the organisation?

When we have a leader who thinks everyone is there to serve him and treats them with a 'hired hands' attitude, thinking only about his own prosperity, what do we feel about him? Contrast this with what happens when we are led by someone who genuinely cares about us and has our best interests in mind and at heart? We are very likely to *exceed expectations.* True leaders know where the credit belongs when the applause comes.

This sort of genuine humility does not rule out confidence.

In fact it creates a new type of boldness. It is less about posturing and more about genuine charisma. Charisma was originally a religious term, meaning 'of the spirit' or 'inspired'. It's about an invisible sparkle in people that money cannot buy.

REFLECT

1. Think back for a few moments on your last week at work. Was there something you saw beyond the ordinary and mundane? Did you follow your values? Ask yourself:

   - Am I a positive force in this office?
   - Do I help people feel good about themselves or am I always pulling them down? See what happens when you act as if your actions really make a difference to those in your office.

- If I were the most important leader in this office, what would I be doing?

2. Think about empowering others. It doesn't matter if others become more successful than you. What is important is that you define and value your own personal vision of success.

3. Identify someone you admire who is a leader in your work, family or community:

- What skills or attitude do they demonstrate that you particularly like?
- Which of these skills do you possess or could you develop?
- What steps will you take over the next month to develop these skills?

4. Write your own acceptance speech for a leadership award. Read it out loud in front of an imaginary audience.

5. Say a thank you blessing to all the mentors and role models you have in your life. Remind yourself that all the wisdom, courage, integrity and strength of your mentors lies within you too.

CHAPTER SEVEN

Entrepreneurs Make A Difference

"In terms of power and influence, you can forget the church, forget politics. There is no more powerful institution in society than business – I believe it is now more important than ever before for business to assume a moral leadership. The business of business should not be about money, it should be about responsibility. It should be about public good, not private greed."

Anita Roddick, founder of The Body Shop

The universe always supports our integrity. This is why spiritual companies are more functional than unethical ones. Sure, you can run a profitable business with the ethics of a rogue. But you will always have to watch your back, fend off investigations, and never know when the dodgy deeds will catch up with you. You can also run a profitable business with the state-of-the-art spiritual agenda, bask in the goodwill of your raving clients, enjoy the harmony at work and earn a great public image. Spirituality is good for you and good for business.

A corporate culture that, for example, even tacitly permits the production of medication with seriously debilitating side effects, needs to be changed. The same can be said for a school which does not endeavour to educate every student. In these cases we must discern what to change and seek the courage to change it. If you are in the lucky position of running your own business, you are free to mould and shape that entity in any way you want. However, employees at all levels of an organisation have the power to influence.

Hindu tradition spells out the consequences of doing harm with *Karma*, the universal law of cause and effect. What goes around, comes around. The only uncertainty is the precise form the effect will take and how soon it will manifest in your life. So why not start playing our part in bringing about that better world rather than devoting our energy to finding ways of getting away with things. Personally, I would love to live in a world where people refrain from doing things not because they're afraid they'll get caught, but simply because they are wrong.

Start to make choices that go beyond a simple material transaction. For example, if you are considering placing an advertisement in a journal, consider whether you want to be identified with the ethos of that particular publication. If you are in PR, check that what you are promoting on behalf of your clients is in line with your ethics. What impact is your business having on the environment and what choices can you make to improve this picture? It may be something as simple as being less wasteful. Discern your role in a greater framework and not only the monetary cost to you. When choosing your dentist, doctor, accountant, lawyer, hairdresser and so on, ascertain whether they share your personal values. Remember you have a choice to work with people who can bring out the best in you.

It is inspiring to see that some corporate leaders can see past personal gain and recognise that our businesses must stand for something beyond profit. A prime example is Body Shop founder Anita Roddick who has addressed health and environmental problems, as well as poverty in the Third World, through innovative strategies. Products are made of non-polluting ingredients manufactured without cruelty to animals, and shops are opened in poor areas to provide employment and return profit to the community.

THE EARTH HOUSEHOLD

There are now over six billion of us on this planet and whilst we are more culturally fragmented, we are also more interconnected. Everything is both global and local – *everywhere.* The body of our planet is a living organism (called 'gaia' by the ancients) and all economic interactions from the individual to the international take place within this moving energy. If circulation through the system is blocked through manipulation, hoarding or fraud, then all parts of the organisation suffer. When there is free circulation of goods, resources and services throughout the gaia, nourishing all parts of the system, then the whole flourishes.

Economics literally means 'earth household'. If we care for the planetary economy as we would our own household, we can see that it must work for all members or it will not work in the long term. Just as we wouldn't tear our house apart to make a fire to keep warm or dump nuclear waste in our gardens, so we must respect the larger household as our own. We must do right and understand the effect of our actions on future generations who will inhabit the earth. Let's stop being a real pain in the ass for our planet!

We are the only species that makes unusable waste; the animal kingdom only makes things that can be used by others. We need to pay attention to Mother Nature – she has got it perfectly in order. I was so heartened to learn that many scientists want to create ingenious products with this in mind. A company has designed an ice cream wrapper that degrades within hours. In an article by Elisabeth Debold for the March 2005 issue of *What Is Enlightenment* magazine, Dr Michael Braungart of McDonough Braungart Design Chemistry says: "But the nice thing is that it is not just biodegradable. That's the minimum. Because the ice-cream packaging contains seeds from rare plants, by throwing it away, you're supporting biodiversity like every songbird does". Man-made waste becomes a nutrient – how remarkable!

Yet humanity as a whole still has a long way to travel up this particular learning curve. Bound by restrictive legislation, many western companies go to countries like China to produce low quality products much more cheaply with lower environmental standards. These products – for example toys made out of plasticizers that give off sterility-causing gases when children chew on them – are true weapons of mass destruction.

The constant rush to market new products has transformed the quality of our lives. Sony launches three new products per hour and 70% of Hewlett Packard's revenue comes from products that didn't exist last year. Such is the power of the corporate juggernaut. At the same time this demand, propelled by the profit motive, has caused atrocious damage to this planet and its inhabitants.

Debold highlights that the biggest soft drinks companies are under scrutiny from watchdog organisations for water pollution and for creating 'opportunity' from water scarcity. In its Coca-Cola profile the Polaris Institute quotes from the company's 1993 annual report: "All of us in the Coca-Cola family wake up each morning knowing that every single one of the world's 5.6 billion people will get thirsty that day. If we make it impossible for these 5.6 billion people to escape Coca-Cola, then we assure our future success for many years to come. Doing anything less is not an option."

Further, Brian Bacon of the Oxford Leadership Academy is quoted as saying: "Short-term profit drives large corporations to buy up small companies and inventions that 'threaten' them with potentially costly change – and then do nothing with the inventions themselves. It's the reason Pfizer, which has substantial community service programs, invests little or nothing in attempting to cure simple diseases that kill millions worldwide, like malaria and tuberculosis, but will invest an enormous amount researching baldness because they can make a killing by selling its 'cure' to the affluent."

Well-intentioned business leaders can find they are prevented from being morally responsible. Bob Hinckley was formerly a partner at the prestigious law firm Skadden Arps, but took a break from his practice after realising the painful truth of this. "I am suggesting that the corporate law be changed to say: 'The duty of directors henceforth shall be to make money for the shareholders *but not at the expense of the environment, human rights, public health and safety, dignity of employees, and the welfare of the communities in which the company operates'*".

Hinckley points out that companies are capable of side-stepping the legal system through well-financed lobbying to create the rules they are happy with. Sometimes they aggressively flout the law; because they have the funds to engage in long legal battles which they can afford to lose.

A strong lobby is needed for the radical change Hinckley proposes, whereby companies will be accountable for their effects on the environment and committed to find better ways to innovate in line with nature. We need to shift our consciousness away from the mechanistic mindset that invented the company. It is this mindset that created our sense of separation from each other.

Today the haves and the have-nots are brushing shoulders throughout the globe and a new pressure is building up. What would it take to stop the destructiveness of these gargantuan entities? Remember, organisations don't change – people do. The question is, is there the willingness?

Many of today's companies are morally and creatively asleep. But you and I can wake them. Imagine what it would be like to go to work each morning for a company that really put consumers first and saw your passions and your idealism as what will take you forward to success. By reinventing capitalism and infusing our own souls into the machine, we can raise the stakes for human possibility.

We know that many companies have amassed resources and power that rival those of certain third-world nations. That is why big business can do so much – in fact I'd say that *business is the most powerful force on this planet.*

SO YOU THINK IT WON'T PAY TO BE NICE?

In their 1997 book *Built to Last,* James Collins and Jerry Porras identified eighteen visionary companies that, between 1926 and 1990, achieved a growth in shareholder value 15 times greater than the general market. Their research shows that contrary to business school doctrine, maximising shareholder wealth was not the main driving force of these visionary companies.

They had tended to pursue a cluster of objectives, of which making money was only one - and not necessarily the primary one. Visionary companies had objectives that transcended purely economic considerations. The majority of their objectives (44%) concerned well-being, and only 20% concerned corporate fitness. Surprisingly, only 6% of the objectives mentioned corporate survival (profits or shareholder value). Some of the more inspiring statements adopted by these companies were:

"We are in the business of preserving and improving human life."

"People are the source of our strength."

"Improving the quality of life through technology and innovation."

"People are number one—treat them well, expect a lot, and the rest will follow."

"Corporate social responsibility."

"Honesty and integrity."

US retailer Whole Foods is a shining example of ethical entrepreneurship. Says co-president Walter Robb: "We're not retailers who have a mission – we're missionaries who retail. At the very heart and soul of Whole Foods is the mission. We're here to make a real difference in people's health and well-being, in the health and well being of the planet, and in creating a workplace based on love and respect." Robb adds that the company is "willing to take steps to change things. We've got to take concrete steps to show not only our own team members, but also the world, that we are serious about our principles."

For example, the company stopped selling sea bass, one of its top-selling fish, when it discovered it was not being fished in a sustainable manner. Despite an explicit policy of putting customers and staff before shareholders, the company has delivered a 25% compounded annual growth rate. "Our return on invested capital is north of thirty-five percent," says Robb. "Those are some of the strongest numbers in the history of food retailing."

Austrian philosopher Rudolf Steiner coined the term 'associative economics'. He said that unless you could link the consumer, the producer, and the distributor of the services into the same organisation, you would always have false economics that would pit those different parties against each other in a win-lose situation. "Whereas if you create [...] structures designed to optimise the whole – all three parts – then you can do things that are miraculous, because you can move money around for the benefit of the whole as opposed to the benefit of only one part."

There is now a payment card, the Interra, which rewards the purchaser for supporting businesses that have holistic values and also takes a small payment off each transaction to donate to a cause the purchaser supports. Greg Stetenpohl, co-founder of the Interra Project says: "We asked what could be a structure...that would allow the values of sustainability and cooperative activity to be built into whatever we do? What if we formed a membership that included both businesses and consumers? And what if we created a movement that could shift the flow of dollars toward those places in society that would do the most good?"

Joseph Jaworski, founder of Generon Consulting, author, lawyer and successful entrepreneur, was deeply inspired by spiritual leader, Dadi Janki of the Brahma Kumaris organisation, to do all that he possibly could to make a difference. His approach is unique. He brings together a group of individuals who represent a microcosm of the whole system. In the child nutrition program for instance, this group might include a mother in a village, local clerics, program officers from CARE as well as local and international business people involved in the food industry.

They start with the premise and honest acceptance that each of them has a different role in creating the system that is the problem. The aim is to get them totally engaged and committed to resolve the issue. The group learn about the real issues by actually going to those places around the world where the problem is most acute. They also engage in spiritual practices designed to take them into a deeper encounter with their purpose assisting them to become an instrument of powerful change. It just takes that one person to really care and be willing to make him or herself available for this process.

YOUR STAFF – THE LIFE FORCE OF YOUR BUSINESS

My years as an executive coach have taught me that employees so often feel unseen and unheard. What most people really want is to feel that they are a part of something. That it matters that they show up at work and give their best and that someone notices when they do, not just when they don't.

As Joe Tye wrote in his book, *Staying On Top: When The World's Upside Down:* "Spirituality is a taboo subject in many organisations. In the long run, it is those organisations able to tap into the tremendous power of personal spiritual strength that will succeed in the marketplace." When the individual is connected to the organisation, people become connected to something deeper – the desire to contribute to a larger purpose, to feel they are part of a greater whole. As this develops, we begin to openly acknowledge the need for others, to see our interdependence, and our desire to belong. Our tribal instinct awakens.

More and more top performers are poised to move jobs in a bid to revitalise their personal development plans as economic confidence grows. At any given time, around 20% of the workforce is looking for another job. And recruitment experts estimate that there will always be 60% open to offer.

Apart from the damage to the business, the cost of departures is huge: between one-and-a-half and three times annual salary. It means large companies need a retention strategy rather than hastily adding a few 'bolt-ons' such as fun days or other events to boost morale. Companies need to develop a culture where all staff members are recognised, not only the key players.

Positive support and genuine acknowledgement can significantly improve performance and can make the difference between valued workers staying or leaving. Can your company afford to take the attitude that says 'We're too busy to deal with feelings"? Consider the time, productivity and money lost when problems escalate to litigation, or when we work with a simmering tension. It doesn't take a great deal of effort to start implementing spiritual standards into business. There isn't a large capital investment, it won't mean upgrading equipment, expanding the facilities, or creating a 'spirituality committee.' What it will take is:

- a willing management to be the *active* role models for the company
- creation of and publicity for a solid mission statement incorporating spiritual standards
- training of current and future employees in implementing the mission statement

Okay, the last one does involve some expense, but the payoff can be tremendous. Look around at the companies that are doing the best during recent economic downturns. The most successful ones are those with high employee and customer loyalty, brought about by a strong management team that focuses on treating everyone fairly, offering win/win situations, and setting the example of 'do unto others...' In other words, they are companies that embody a spiritual leadership model.

Vodafone has encouraged retention by offering staff a comprehensive menu of personal-development opportunities. Their Global Leadership programme, for example, puts talented managers through a development scheme that includes coaching, mentoring and participation in an MBA programme. Staff can transfer to other parts of the company to gain experience or study for professional qualifications. They are encouraged to submit their own development plans.

More and more companies are realising that to retain their life force they will need to cater to the higher needs of employees. Our old ways of doing business are falling away and being replaced by a growing recognition that the contribution itself is what matters – and you can contribute and have fun at the same time! We are learning that we do not need to do 'serious' things, seriously. That work can be play, and that play can be extremely productive and fun.

Sonia Stojanovic, in conjunction with McKinsey and Co., created a program that took more than 21,000 employees through personal development workshops. In addition to changing how people related to each other at work, the results were dramatic. ANZ Bank, previously the least preferred employer in Australian financial services, is now the employer of choice. Staff satisfaction increased by 35% in four years. The bank has won 'Australian Bank of the Year' for three years running and its stock price has more than doubled.

For Stojanovic, the secret of the success comes from tapping into the intrinsically human longing for meaning and wholeness: "We're giving people hope – the hope to find meaning and to not compartmentalise their lives into home, work and self. We're inviting people to ask the questions: Why am I here? What is my contribution? How can the work I'm doing and the service I'm providing bring forth the best I can be in every moment? People really want to feel that what they are doing is being counted and is contributing to the success of the organisation as well as to the greater good. They are concerned about sustainability and future generations."

REFLECT

1. If it were up to you, how would you create positive change at your workplace?

2. How would you begin to close the gulf between rich and poor?

3. What would you do to relieve our struggling ecosystem?

4. How is your company meeting your needs for a larger purpose? Is our consciousness more evolved outside the office than in it?

5. Think of ways to shift from a sales mentality to a service mentality. How would you behave?

6. For the next fortnight challenge yourself to strike the word 'I' from your vocabulary. Don't be surprised if you start to feel a bit uneasy – it's the ego that is shrinking and feeling sorry for itself!

And for those who run businesses:

1. Consider appointing a committee to explore how spirituality might impact your workplace, customers and productivity.

2. At your next staff meeting, ask people: "What's it really like for you to work here? What's it like when you wake up on Monday morning, and know that it's time to come back to work?" And then listen, not only with your ears, but also with your heart and soul.

3. Now ask yourself these questions:

- Are the people who work for me growing?
- Are they healthier or less healthy as a result of how they spend their working lives?
- Are they being paid a just and reasonable wage?

PART TWO

TRANSFORMATION

CHAPTER EIGHT

The Clearing

"It is only when we have the courage to face things without any self-deception or illusion that a light will develop out of events by which the path to success may be recognized."

I Ching or the Book of Changes

Transformation is not a process, it is a *willingness*. It is now time to take an honest look at what's been holding you back and how you are going to move forward in your life. Through my coaching practice I have helped people from all rungs of the corporate ladder, from secretaries and graduate trainees to company directors and entrepreneurs. And over the years I've noticed the same obstacles coming up again and again for people.

The next three chapters take you through those obstacles on the path to career fulfilment, and how to get over, under or around them. It is a distillation of the work I have done with my clients and you will find many real-life case studies showing how these principles have worked for people from all walks of life. I've divided the possible challenges you may be facing into three categories.

The first chapter of this section takes you through the ways you could be sabotaging yourself. Perhaps you are holding yourself back through limiting beliefs, counterproductive behaviours or poor time management. In the second section we turn our attention to your passion (or otherwise) for your current work. Finally, a look at the external factors of your working life: where you work, who you work with, who manages you and how happy (or otherwise) you are with all of this.

Personal growth is not always easy. In fact, it is one of our greatest challenges. Sometimes we must face our own ugliness. Often we have to become painfully aware of our unproductive values and patterns of behaviour before we are willing to give them up. We must realise the real cost of our unhelpful values and destructive behaviour.

You may notice aspects of yourself in the following examples. If you do notice some familiarity and feel disturbed, please do not be discouraged by this. It may feel bad – this is because you are no longer anaesthetised by being unaware of your behaviour. You are no longer distanced, through denial or disassociation, from your experience. You may be starting to see the truth about the games we all play from time to time. It takes courage – this is often called the path of the spiritual warrior – to endure the sharp pains of discovery rather than choose to take the dull pain of unconsciousness for the rest of your life. It is your choice.

Your task is to know what is really going on within you. We live in a planet of polarity – both negative and positive. Recognise both sides of your nature. Whatever is going on in your environment you are capable of handling and if you do not believe it, it is because you have not looked at your magnificence. The sign of a mature being is one who acknowledges the pull of different energy fields and makes the decision whether to follow a particular energy or not. They see *choices.*

To be a Master you must first be the master of your own life. You become aware that there are areas of your psyche that you have not looked at and these are often reflected as fears. It is like waking up, which means taking everything behind you that you have tried to hide and placing it in your vision. Your inner voice says "I am ready. I want to know, so I can be harmless. I want to be harmless, because it is the only way to move in power on this planet". A true Master is one who has gone into all parts of his psyche, has found it all, and turned away from nothing. All that is presented, is accepted, no matter how seemingly dark. Life then takes on a very different meaning. Then no adversity is unwelcome and divine grace is always by your side. You slip into a space of gratitude, joy and acceptance.

Finish any unfinished business. Address your shadows and keep bringing them into the light, and eventually they will dissipate. Hiding from yourself like this is fighting yourself. The minute you put out the call for change, new energy will start coming, and then you just need to receive it.

When you ask for assistance from anyone in looking at your shadows and fears, be wary of the relationship that turns into dependency. You must always maintain your personal power – only you have the real answers to your problems. No-one knows you better than yourself. The vibrational pattern of a true teacher is one who constantly turns you back on yourself to develop your own inner strengths and intuition.

In helping many of the clients you'll read about in the following pages, I use in part a coaching method known as the GROW model, which I'll now outline briefly.

Step 1: Goal

Coach and client agree on a specific aim, objective or outcome.

Step 2: Reality

Time is taken to look at the circumstances of the client's life, to check assumptions, and to invite honest self-examination.

Step 3: Options

The coach elicits suggestions from the client by asking effective questions and guides him/her towards decisions.

Step 4: Way forward

Coach and client commit to action, define a timeframe for their objectives, and identify how to overcome obstacles.

CHAPTER NINE

Get Out Of Your Own Way

"Try not to become a man of success but rather try to become a man of value."

Albert Einstein

Gremlins pop up sometimes and we need to tame them. Gremlins sabotage our best laid plans and often they tell us that we shouldn't try anything different in case we fail or make a fool of ourselves. When no-one is looking – have a go at saying stop! Our core beliefs that run our lives often sound like this: 'I can't do that – I'm not good enough'. In order to gain freedom from these drivers we need to take full responsibility for all the events that have happened to us. Give up the 'why me' story and transform it into 'this is my journey and I needed to learn some key lessons from this'. This is the place of power from which you can alter your reality. Create an internal dialogue that empowers you.

Journaling is a good tool to identify any gremlins. The focus is on forgiveness and expressing what is holding you back without judgment. Also, we can use our body to lead our brain. As soon as a negative comment comes into your mind, change your body posture to the way you would stand if you were feeling strong and confident. You can also imagine the negative thought as a comically ridiculous voice or cartoon character. That will distance you from their impact.

Do you want it bad enough to face your fears? Start by changing your internal statements to questions, for example: 'I am bored stiff of my job' to: 'Could I be excited by my job?'; 'I make no difference to the organisation' becomes 'Could I make a difference to the organisation?'. Our need to play small or stay safe prevents us from committing fully to our lives. Would you prefer to stay in a job you hate or risk creating a business you absolutely love? Would you rather be right about feeling powerless or be wrong about your ability to surpass your wildest expectations of yourself?

If you knew you had six months to live would you continue what you are doing now?

Say to yourself: I am worthy of having what I desire and I am going to do whatever it takes to fulfil my aspirations. Let the universe guide you towards this now. When you become focused about your direction, the universe collaborates to meet your needs in what may seem to be mere coincidences. The eminent psychologist, Carl Jung, termed this as 'Synchronicity'. If you are mindful of these circumstances, you will progress in leaps and bounds. I encourage my clients to open their eyes to this remarkable phenomenon.

Keeping your word is so important for change. Even if it is a small task like making a list of things to do everyday, if you don't do it you are telling the universe and yourself that you cannot be counted on. Breaking our promises wears down our self respect. Treat your word like gold and it will deliver gold. If you are not going to do it, don't say it.

Is it worth it to invest your time and energy to achieve your dreams? This is your decision to make – there is no magic carpet ride to wherever you want to be in your life. Everything you need to change already lies within you. Take small significant steps and you will see the payoff. Analyse your excuses. Do they hinder your progress to achieving your dreams?

Do you feel anxious when someone tells you to go with the flow, maybe lighten up a bit? Do you like to hold on with a tight grip to feel in control? Often the last thing we can imagine doing is becoming passive as there is a strong belief in our culture that you have to achieve and be doing things to be powerful. Passive energy has its own kind of strength. Surrender is not weakness or loss. It is powerful non-resistance which gives birth to our higher self.

Whenever I go past a cemetery I look at the stones representing those that were once living with cares, worries, ambitions, losses and bad hair days and ask myself: 'Where are they now?' It reminds me to ask myself: 'What's important to me in this moment? What is vital to me now?' It doesn't matter if you are stuck as long as you are happy to be alive. Only people who have suffered enough emotionally realise that it is the self that perpetuates all emotional suffering. Get out of your own way.

If you are a boss you will want your workers to do their best work for you and not burn effigies of you behind your back! Recognise workers as human beings, not as machines. Lao Tsu advised leaders to demonstrate humanity, compassion and mercy as signs of strength. We've been trained to be tough and go-getting and to look upon gentleness as the soft side where you are vulnerable. The Tao on the other hand teaches that the true sign of strength is that you can afford to be gentle. The golden rule – respect, both yourself and others.

If you find your staff are not being creative or acting autonomously maybe you need to consider whether they are always being told what to do. Instead try giving directional guidance and coaching them so that they have the space to grow, express themselves and deliver their ideas on time.

OBSTACLE 1

"I'm so stressed, but if I relax I'll lose my edge and fail"

Are you so busy that you never have time to slow down, breathe deeply and enjoy life? Are you in fact afraid to slow down because you've told yourself that you can't afford to? Or perhaps you have convinced yourself that you thrive on the adrenalin? If this is you, then I'm willing to bet that your stress is an avoidance tactic; a distraction to keep your mind busy so that it does not focus on the things you'd rather remain in denial about.

In this way, workaholism can become a form of escape. But remember: no one ever escaped their way to fulfilment, so it is important to become conscious again. Just recognising this pattern at work is a big step in the right direction. Consider if you are the sort of person who only feels okay when they are running around in some kind of conflict. Stop and take time to really see what is going on in your life. Allow your instinct to tell you what needs to be done – this requires some quiet reflection time.

CASE STUDY

Jill was a company director in her early forties. She ran a small financial consultancy which provided specialist training to staff in investment banks. She was not making as much money as she wanted, yet she was rushed off her feet and could not see how she could try any harder than she already was. Her life and business were both in chaos and she was lurching from one crisis to the next. The problem Jill was having is one I often see in people who have started businesses. Jill was very gifted at what she *did* – understanding complex financial concepts and teaching them to others – but she was not gifted at *managing*. In fact, she did not have a clue how to manage her staff, her time *or* her finances.

The crunch had come when she was about to start a two-day training course at a leading bank and she was still in the office at 9.00 pm the night before with her slide presentation unfinished, yelling at her assistant.

When she first came to see me, Jill was convinced her problem stemmed from the fact there simply were not enough hours in the day. So I got Jill to keep a diary for the next two weeks, noting exactly how she spent her time. It was enlightening to say the least.

At our next session, I helped Jill to divide all her activities into four categories. The most effective time management models I've seen use variations of these same distinctions:

- Urgent and important (must be done and must be done now).
- Urgent but not important (those things that interrupt us and take us away from our true objectives).
- Important but not urgent (the more time a person spends on activities in this category, the more fulfilled they will be. It can involve work or non-work activities; ideally there should be a mix of the two).

- Not important and not urgent (Mindless activities like watching rubbish on TV. US motivational speaker Tony Robbins calls this 'the zone of escape').

Categories one and three include all the important activities. This is where successful, fulfilled people spend most of their time. Remember: 'important' does not necessarily mean 'work-related', although items in category one usually are. It could mean taking a scuba-diving course in Mauritius if that is what fires you, or learning to salsa dance. You are in the zone of fulfilment whenever you are following your passions and growing as a person.

Categories two and four are the thieves of fulfilment. However, the majority of people squander away their lives in these zones. And I was unsurprised to learn, on looking at Jill's diary, that this was where she had been spending almost all of her time. An example of 'urgent but not important', the zone in which Jill spent most of her time, is having your computer set up to interrupt you with a 'ding' every time an e-mail comes in. And stopping whatever you are doing to answer every e-mail. This was one of the habits Jill admitted to.

She also allowed herself to get held up on long and unproductive phone-calls, even at times when she was already late meeting a client deadline. Jill was an action illusionist: because she was always busy she assumed she must be achieving things. Yet the most important things in her life and business were not being done, simply because she never gave herself time to do them.

After that session I got Jill to carry on with her diary, but this time with a constant consciousness of whether what she was doing was leading her towards fulfilment or away from it. This new-found awareness led to a gradual shift away from the time-wasting activities and towards productive ones. Jill had freed up a great deal of time, and it had knock-on effects throughout her life and business. For example, because she now felt less rushed she not only treated her employees better; she was also able to set aside time to learn about managing people.

REFLECT

Do you thrive on being busy but feel anxious any time it is just you alone with your thoughts? The more uncomfortable you feel sitting in silence with your thoughts, the more important it is that you slow down. When you are centred you become part of the solution.

OBSTACLE 2

"I'm afraid to leave my comfort zone!"

Do you lack confidence? Are you afraid of being different; of taking a stand and being noticed? Do you have difficulty expressing yourself at work? Are you so afraid of making a mistake that your creativity is smothered, and you are valuing what people think of you over what you know you are contributing?

The comfort zone is all about certainty: it is an attachment to what is familiar, secure and comfortable coupled with a fear of the unknown. We all need some certainty in our lives. However, I firmly believe that the less certainty you can live with, the greater your quality of life will be. Sadly, most people need a great deal of certainty. In their pursuit of this they miss out on all manner of exciting opportunities and new experiences.

Can you imagine what it would be like to be fearless? To embrace new challenges, situations and people with joyful enthusiasm and curiosity instead of with miserable fear and suspicion?

CASE STUDY

Raj came to me with a common problem. He is a computer analyst. He was desperate to break out of his rut and take on challenges, but was paralysed with fear. For example, his head was buzzing with ideas, yet in every staff meeting he sat silent, afraid to open his mouth for fear of sounding stupid. In fact, his only goal during meetings was to avoid getting called on to speak, so he spent them avoiding eye contact with anyone. All this was having a limiting effect on the projects he was given to work on. He also suspected it was one of the reasons he kept getting passed over for promotion. That and his underlying belief that he was not as 'clever' as his highly qualified colleagues.

The first thing we looked at was why he felt that what he had to contribute would be stupid or unwelcome. It was the first time he had ever questioned this. What was he gaining by not sharing his views?

What was certain was that he was losing a lot more than he was gaining. He soon realised that what he called his comfort zone was in fact not comfortable at all. He was tired of playing small and wasting his potential.

I got him to visualise himself speaking up and his colleagues and superiors being impressed with his ideas – ideas which turned out to be extremely valuable to the company. I also got him to identify a role model; the person he would most like to emulate in this area. When breaking through old habits and building better ones it can be very helpful to have someone to model. He chose Richard Branson for his bold, innovative brilliance. He imagined how Branson would act sitting at the boardroom table: what would his body language be like, how would he voice his ideas? He also imagined Branson cheering him on and patting him on the back after he delivered his ideas!

The first time Raj spoke up it was easier than he thought it would be and he was delighted with the response he got. He was suddenly on the radar of his superiors, and as a result he was given the responsibility he knew he could handle. When Raj and I parted ways, it was with him feeling confident that next time there was an opening for someone at his level of the company to be moved to the next, he stood a great chance. He also realised that courage is often better rewarded than qualifications and a high I.Q.

Hypnosis harnesses our natural mental ability to deeply immerse our imagination in an experience, so that we can learn to overcome fears and rehearse skills as Raj had done.

REFLECT

"*Comfort starts as a servant and becomes a master*" Kahlil Gibran

Comfort zones slowly paralyse us, but we get so used to hanging out there that we don't feel the stiffness until much later. Hindu and Buddhist philosophy maintain that permanence and security are illusions. Illusions never turn into something real and can often breed attraction in the grasping mind – as well as false desires which ultimately lead to suffering.

We all know how quickly pleasure can turn into pain. It's easy to get attached even to negative things – the devil you know. Change is the only constant. If you think that the best times are behind you, then they probably are. As Anais Nin observed: "We don't see things as they are, we see things as we are". Focus on your future – you have your whole life ahead of you. Expect good things to happen. When things turn out in your favour, see it as a part of a wider pattern of events. This will help you in times of difficulty. How often do you try new things? Think of new ways you can open up your world to new possibilities.

OBSTACLE 3

"I'm driven by winning at all costs"

Do you focus mainly on your reputation? Is being known, being highly successful and having powerful influence very important to you? Are you good at psychological warfare, taking unfair advantage of others' weakness? Do you want to win at all costs and you have no qualms about manipulating things to appear powerful? One-upmanship and power control can be addictive emotions. The results are always short-lived.

CASE STUDY

Andrew was a lawyer in his fifties. Although he was highly competent in court and in front of clients, he was a disaster at managing his staff. His sharp intellect may have been an asset in the court room, but in the office he used it as a weapon. He had gained a reputation as a bully, though he did not know this until he was faced with some feedback from staff. When his superiors presented him with his first 360-degree appraisal – something his firm had recently introduced – he was stunned. His subordinates were almost without exception very unhappy with the way he was managing them. And one member of staff had even written that she was ashamed to work for him.

When Andrew reflected on his behaviour at work, he realised the comments were justified. But this was the first time he had ever considered how his work persona might affect others. When he came to see me, it was to find out how he could change for the better. He had no idea where to start. First we needed to look at how he'd got into these negative patterns in the first place. He had no real joy in his life, he confided. It was as if he was under a cloud of anxiety all the time. He took this out on others. He also had a guiding belief that he had to be on the offensive at all times; if he let his guard down and took a softly-softly approach he would lose his edge.

I got him to examine these statements one by one – to hold each up to the light of inquiry – and see how true they were. Gradually, Andrew realised that the very defence mechanisms he thought were protecting him were actually sabotaging him. He would be much more effective at work if he was able to interact with his staff in a way which got them on his side and got the best out of them. Similarly, if he made relaxation a priority so that he wasn't always on a knife-edge of stress, he would do his own work more effectively.

The 360-degree appraisal was Andrew's initial catalyst for change, and he used it as a powerful motivating factor. He was determined that the next appraisal – six months after the first – would be a very different matter altogether.

REFLECT

See how you do at this quiz:

1. Name the five wealthiest people in the world.
2. Name the last five winners of the Miss World contest.
3. Name five people who have won the Nobel or Pulitzer Prize.
4. Name the last five Academy Award winners for best actor and actress.

How did you do?

Here's another quiz. See how you do on this one:

1. List a few teachers who aided your journey through school.
2. Name three friends who have helped you through a difficult time.
3. Name five people who have taught you something worthwhile.
4. Think of a few people who have made you feel appreciated and special.

The moral is we remember what is personal and important to us and besides over time applause and achievements fade away. Don't be surprised if you feel like writing a few thank you notes after the second quiz!

CHAPTER TEN

The Emerging Force Within

"Success is not the key to happiness. Happiness is the key to success. If you love what you are doing, you will be successful."

Albert Schweitzer

If you feel your work or life are lacking in meaning and purpose you are not alone. In fact, so many people have this experience that it has come to seem almost normal. Yet few are truly happy living this way. Our time here is precious – literally irreplaceable.

Many of my clients find it helpful during our sessions to talk and reflect about their purpose and the meaning they attach to their work. Most realise that current uncertainty about their purpose is not the same as having a purposeless life. Consider a man who, looking back on his life after 66 years, thought he was a failure: Winston Churchill. He was a soldier, journalist, parliamentarian and author before he was 25. He held a wide variety of powerful positions in government but felt worthless because he had failed to attain the office of prime minister.

His time came, of course. Hindsight being 20/20 we can see that his earlier experiences were a necessary preparation for the highest office and that he would not have been the great leader he was if this responsibility had been granted to him before he was ready for it. You don't jump from nowhere to somewhere. You are always somewhere. Even if you don't want to be where you are now it is still a point on your path. You may feel you have missed your calling, but you may not realise you are exactly where you are supposed to be at this point in time. You just don't see the links yet. You may be engaged in something crucially important for you without realising it.

All of us move towards our calling in stages, taking with us all the resources we have accumulated over the years. There is no substitute for constant inner exploration. We do not always discover ourselves in a blinding flash of insight. But we can start right here, right now.

Madeleine Albright preceded her monumental political career with being a mother, charity fundraiser and getting a PhD. She brought with her a range of well-honed, transferable skills. These skills we sometimes overlook when looking at what options we have to find fulfilling work. Developing passion is a process of transition – it is not about making rash knee-jerk decisions where we expect instant approval for our plans to be the next Lakshmi Mittal, the steel billionaire. Doing what you love doesn't have to involve years of training – it can even happen out of apparent disaster.

Are you bored? This is a common consequence of lack of purpose. No one is bored in a crisis. In a disaster, everyone has a purpose: self-preservation. The psychologist Abraham Maslow's hierarchy of needs describes five different levels of human need, each building on the last. At the bottom are the 'physiological' needs; if we do not have food, water, air and shelter all our efforts go to securing these until we do.

At the next level are the 'safety' needs: finding stability and consistency in a chaotic world. Levels three and four are our needs for love and esteem, and it is only with the foundation of these four that we can reach the fifth level: self-actualisation, which Maslow described as: "Becoming more and more what one is. Becoming everything one is capable of being." It is at this level that attention turns to the search for knowledge, peace, self-fulfilment, oneness with God and so on.

While in one sense having everything you need and want in the material world is a luxury enjoyed by only a fraction of people, it is a double-edged sword. The feeling of having no more mountains to climb can be debilitating. Alexander The Great supposedly wept because he had no more worlds to conquer.

I'm not recommending you create crisis to keep yourself stimulated! Do you really need regular brushes with death in order to feel alive? No. Spiritual work presents you with internal mountains to climb. However, sometimes we need to rip back to the wild to refresh ourselves. Whatever reconnects you to the natural world is the surest way to regain perspective. It rekindles an appreciation of life itself. Understanding that life is a great gift and enjoying all the things you do – these are great antidotes to purposelessness.

However, the best way of all to counteract feelings of emptiness is to help someone else. At work, this could mean taking a real interest in and supporting your trainees.

In his book, *The Power of Now*, Eckhart Tolle talks about the concept of 'waiting': "Give up waiting as a state of mind. When you catch yourself slipping into waiting, snap out of it. Come into the present moment. Just be, and enjoy being. If you are present, there is never any need for you to wait for anything. So next time somebody says: "I'm sorry to have kept you waiting," you can reply, "That's all right, I wasn't waiting I was just standing here enjoying myself – in joy in myself."“

OBSTACLE 1

"My job does not inspire me enough"

Do you feel that you have missed your true vocation in life? Are you just showing up at the office each day to pay the mortgage, with no real passion for your work? Does the clock move slowest of all during working hours? Are your work goals personally fulfilling, or are they just to please your boss or earn you a commission? Remember you are also competing against people who love their work and if you are only working for the money you are likely to be blown away by the competition. Dedication shines every time.

CASE STUDY

Gianni was an accountant in his mid-thirties. He was quite happy at work, but what he really wanted to be, he told me, was a chef. He loved experimenting with food and creating new dishes, and friends and family had told him that he had real talent. He was an avid reader of cookery books and would travel miles on expeditions to find rare ingredients. As this passion increased, he felt more and more certain that he should give up his job and open a restaurant. He needed no training, he assured me at our first session; he already knew how to cook! He envisaged himself in charge and at the creative helm, just like he was in his kitchen at home.

So I got him to do some detailed research into what he would have to do to make his dream a reality. What he discovered shocked him. Gianni had had a romantic notion that he could borrow a modest amount of money to open a restaurant on a shoe-string and then expand into somewhere bigger and better. However, his research showed him just how competitive the restaurant business is, and what a financial risk he would be taking. As the bank would use his house as collateral against any loan, he decided that it was too risky to take this route to becoming a chef, especially as he had a wife and two young children.

This left him with the option of undertaking formal chef's training and then working his way up the ranks in restaurant and hotel kitchens, starting, of course, in the lowliest positions. The thought of spending weeks peeling potatoes did not appeal; nor was this option much better from a financial perspective. While he was training he would use up most of savings as he'd still have to support his family, and initially he would earn a fraction of what he now earned as an accountant. And in the harsh, competitive world of the restaurant kitchen there was no guarantee he would ever reach his current salary. In addition, not only would he have to work longer hours; they were also considerably less sociable hours, as anyone who is serious about success in the restaurant business must kiss goodbye to evenings, weekends and holidays.

This exercise helped Gianni get clarity that although cooking was his passion, it did not need to be his career. Once Gianni was clear about this, he was free to begin fully indulging his passion right away. He decided how much time he'd like to be able to spend on it every week, and scheduled this in his diary, making it a priority. And he made his next holiday a cookery course in Italy!

Coaching guided Gianni to the realisation that he could live his passion outside of his career, but for many it has the opposite outcome: it is the catalyst that finally gives them the courage to take the brave step they have needed to take for a long time.

Doing what you love will often offer you greater prosperity in the long term, but sometimes it won't. Sometimes when you do what you really enjoy, you *need* less money.

REFLECT

Finding meaning is an ongoing challenge. Think about the inevitable passage of time and your best use of it. Unguarded time slips away. Find meaning in the small moments of ordinary life, rather than just wasting them. Use anything that comes your way for your personal evolution. Living this way allows us to be more than we would otherwise have been. It is about being fully present in every moment, even if you are just filing some papers. For evolution requires an engagement with, not a withdrawal from, life itself. Don't go through the motions – enjoy every meal by tasting each mouthful; talk to a colleague and hear every word. Pay attention to the moments in your life and refuse to live it in a hurry. Affirm to yourself: *I have plenty of time. How long it takes is how long it takes.*

OBSTACLE 2

"I don't know what I want!"

Are you unfulfilled but confused about what it would take to change that? Do you lack a clear picture of what fulfilment would look and feel like for you? Work is a journey for most people. Not everyone leaves school with a clear idea of what their calling is; far from it. But finding your vocation in life is one of the surest ways to fulfilment. You may need to dig a bit for your talents and try many things. How will you know unless you do?

These days most people hold a variety of jobs in different fields during the course of their lives. Some things we need to learn from experience, and that means that sometimes you have to do a job to discover you are not suited to it. You haven't wasted your time as long as you make use of what you've learned when making your next decision.

No matter how long your father has treasured his vision of you making it as a cabinet minister, if rummaging for antiques in car boot sales is more your thing, go ahead and take a part-time job with an auctioneer and a day job to pay the mortgage. You will be living authentically. Besides you are not here to fulfil the dreams of frustrated parents!

Unless you grant yourself the flexibility to pursue different purposes during your life, you could end up like the most popular kid in school still reliving your past glory years twenty years later without a new vision. We are not made to do just one thing. Don't cling to any one thing, stretching it beyond its time. Like overblown bubble gum it may pop. If you have succeeded in the past, no one can take your memories away from you. But they won't last forever. Nothing does.

You can re-live those memories, but you need to let go sometime. You might not find another purpose until you can do this. It isn't easy, which is why we can all relate to the image of the popular kid who can't move on. It's a condition which finds its way into my consulting room regularly. It takes courage to move on. There is some good news here: Carl Jung, believed the greatest potential for growth is in the second half of life. He noticed that to carry on with the same goals we had when we were younger can make us feel rejected and failures. Finding a way to stop looking backwards and to look to who and what we can become is an important step.

Whenever I feel a sense of despondency and miss the cut and thrust of my youth, my father's wise words give me a source of strength that calms me to a more accepting state. He reminds me that the brightest future will always be based on a forgotten past and that I can't move forward in life until I let go of my past disappointments and heartaches. I have spent quiet time assimilating my life's experiences and come to accept myself. By evaluating what beliefs I hold true in my life and putting behind me memories of less-than-perfect behaviour I have found new ways to be comfortable in my own new skin. Shedding the old has led to many unexpected gifts and adventures in my life that I am so grateful for.

CASE STUDY

Rania came to see me because she was going back to work after a 20-year career break during which she had raised three children. Her problem was that she didn't know what she wanted to do. She had been a secretary until the age of 26 when she got married and had her first child. Now she wanted to try something different. But as a woman in her late forties, with little work experience and no qualifications, what were her options? She was terrified that she may become invisible and drop out of view like her mother had in her forties. She still dreamed of making her mark, but felt a little overwhelmed by entering uncharted territory.

So our first task was to brainstorm all the things she enjoyed and was good at. At first we didn't seem to be getting anywhere as Rania initially drew a complete blank. Rania had the look of someone jaded by the disappointments in her life. I encouraged her to start a journal of her dreams. If money was no object and she could not fail, what would she like to do? If she woke up one morning and overnight her fairy godmother had granted her wish, what is the first thing she would notice? This is when her floodgates finally opened. She could think of lots of things that fit these criteria but still nothing really stood out. However, as she reflected further a clear pattern began to emerge. Rania was really interested in anything to do with gardens, plants and flowers.

She had long pursued this as a hobby and had occasionally thought of turning it into a career, but the idea had always been quickly chased out of her mind by self-defeating thoughts. In fact, these same thoughts followed hot on the heels of her bringing up this idea during our session. I got her to look at them logically and see whether they were really true. Was it really true, for example that she was too old to start this new venture, or that she could never make money out of it? Of course not! There were plenty of role models around to contradict this negative thought and in any case I asked Rania to consider the *advantages* of age and she came up with a handful. Her emotional state changed from fear to curiosity and a little excitement! Rania needed hardcore evidence that age was no barrier to starting a new business, so I gave this to her. More than 60% of new successful businesses are in the hands of the over fifties in the U.K. She also realised that her well honed feminine talents of intuition and interpersonal skills are crucial in business.

A few months after she identified her chosen career Rania had researched the market and what it would take to be successful in it. First of all, she'd need professional training. She found a full-time course that would give her the education and expertise needed to turn her passion into a career. I taught Rania to relax during this time when she was naturally a little anxious. She learned some deep breathing methods which helped her to face her fears and to muster up patience. We discussed any obstacles she might face that could slow her down. She made peace with these without fighting them or wishing they would go away. Thinking 'if only' only adds power to the obstacles and takes power away from you.

I taught Rania a visualisation technique to help her entrench her passion where she imagined seeing herself on a movie screen going through the experience of success and accomplish all she wanted flawlessly. The idea is to see this image large, bright and colourful, adding sound, feelings, smells and tastes. I taught her to activate as many of her five senses as possible. For example she could see herself designing award-winning landscape plans on large paper, smelling the roses and freesias which she adored and touching the fresh soil with her rubber gloves. Rania could even hear the accolades she receives from delighted clients and the media! Too right – you must always step up and enjoy the rewards.

There was gratitude written all over her face as she smiled. I saw Rania's body posture literally change in minutes as these powerful changes began to take root right down to the cellular level. She stood tall as she appreciated the results of her efforts. She had come a long way in her mind and it was only a matter of time before this would become her new reality. She saw the new, confident her on the movie screen and I asked her to integrate this new image by stepping into that image and becoming one with this new her.

Rania embraced this technique with a tremendous amount of joy and because she gave herself the permission to overcome her hang-ups, she started to believe that she was very capable of starting her own business. Feeling unstoppable she had tears in her eyes as she thought she had lost this determination over the years. I used an NLP technique called 'Anchoring' which Rania repeated everyday and she reported that she felt a power and strength growing inside as she kept adding more real-life details to the imagery. When something you see, hear or feel, taste or smell consistently changes your state or you consistently respond in the same way, this is an example of anchoring. An example of a visual anchor is a smile; music can be an auditory anchor. They build habits. Rania felt an emotional freedom from being aware of the anchors she had and choosing to respond to the ones she wanted. She kept this resourceful state and after her training she immediately started a landscape gardening business and is also enjoying running weekend courses teaching children about horticulture.

How does it feel to stand in the shoes of an optimist? Try out a new way of seeing the world, a new way of speaking and hearing. What are the possibilities you can create when you ask questions like 'what if' that open doors, rather than the 'why me' which slams the door shut on your face?

REFLECT

Herman Hesse won the Nobel Prize in Literature, but earlier in life he seriously considered suicide. His talent as a writer blossomed later in life, but in the meantime he couldn't see the purpose in his life. However, the difficulties he had faced in his own life, illuminated in his writing, inspired a generation to consider enlightenment and inner meaning. Yet this purpose was lost on him as he struggled in his earlier years. He toughed it out until things got better. If you exercise patience and courage – two cardinal virtues – change will come.

OBSTACLE 3

"I'm driven by financial worries"

Do you find that there is never quite enough money to enable you to live the life you want? Or maybe you *do* have the financial resources to live the life you want, but mortgage, holiday home, car payments and school fees are all conspiring to keep you trapped in a job you dislike.

How many of the things you purchase every day do you really need? Have you ever wondered about that? We have departed so far from our real necessities, that many of us are not even capable of determining the difference between luxury and vital needs. Ask yourself: do I need all this to be happy?

Is there anything wrong with that? Not really…as long as we can afford it, and as long as we realise that all things pass. What you regard as normal today could become luxury for you tomorrow…or the other way around: obsolete. It all depends on how life treats you…or how *you* treat life. The worst thing you can do is to take things for granted: a high-flying job, a six-figure salary, a great spouse, a nice house, or even something as simple as a mobile phone!

CASE STUDY

Richard was the global head of communications at a blue-chip company. In his early forties, he was happily married with four children. "Although, I must admit, not as happily married as I used to be," he confided. Richard hardly ever saw his wife or children as he was working such long hours. And when he was home he was so burnt out that all we wanted to do was sleep or read the papers.

He worked, on average, 60 hours a week, and spent an additional hour a day commuting. He also travelled a lot, sometimes two weeks out of a month. It did not leave much time for his marriage, nor did he have much of a relationship with his children. He was deeply unhappy with this, and so was the rest of the family. When Richard first came to see me it was for advice on how to relax, and how to increase his energy levels. Although he hated his job, changing to a less demanding one wasn't an option for him, he told me. He couldn't afford to. Yet when I quizzed him about this it became clear he did not really have a clue where his money was going. So the first thing I got him to do was to take a really close look at his outgoings.

I explained that I did not need to know his financial business; I just wanted him to review his expenditure and see whether he was right. His four children were in private school, and that cost over £30,000 a year. But that was an essential expense, he told me. Fair enough. As we looked over the rest, it was a different story. He and his family lived in a bigger house than they needed, in one of the more expensive areas of London. They also had a luxury holiday home in France that they rarely visited more than twice a year. Gourmet restaurants, ski trips, astronomical mobile phone bills (especially with four kids). He was, quite simply, haemorrhaging cash.

All of this is fine if you can afford it – afford it meaning, if what you have to do to maintain that lifestyle is leaving you fulfilled, joyful and at peace. Nothing could be further from the truth for Richard. But he was starting to realise he had choices he never knew existed. He went through the family finances with his wife and they realised that he could afford to halve his salary and they would still live very comfortably. It took a while for this to sink in, but what it meant was that the weight hanging round his shoulders for so long was lifted.

After much reflection, Richard ended up taking a more fulfilling job in a smaller company. Not only did he enjoy his hours at work more; he also had a lot more time to devote to other things in his life.

REFLECT

"Many men go fishing all of their lives without knowing that it is not the fish they're after."

Henry David Thoreau

Decide from the outset that you are going to be true to your core values. Pursue your life's purpose with the intention of being the very best you can be, rather than focusing primarily upon financial rewards. You can certainly have a monetary goal. However, just be aware of the danger of letting this become the primary motive. Continually re-assess the balance between your externally-focused activities and your spiritual goals. Never let that balance slip. When we find our true calling and trust that what we put forth from our inner self will be of value to others, we will receive what we need to live in exchange.

CHAPTER ELEVEN

Harmony At Work

"It is amazing what can be accomplished when nobody cares about who gets the credit."

Robert Yates

In any organisation, toxic emotions – negative emotions that 'infect' an environment – can have a significant impact on that organisation's ability to motivate or retain staff. Computer viruses are not the only viruses that spread and cause havoc in the operations of business. We pay far more attention to computer virus attacks and spend a fortune in virus protection programmes but we disregard the other debilitating infections in the workplace.

At work we must learn not to take things personally. All great leaders faced attack and opposition – Jesus, Gandhi, Martin Luther King, to name just a few. It is the *fear* of attack which is the greatest cause of millions of us leading mediocre lives. We would rather do nothing than face being true to ourselves, and take on the responsibility of being a leader. It takes courage to stand out and speak up when others are silent. Facing an attack often helps you discover an untapped inner strength. In the midst of criticism ask yourself this: am I acting with integrity and responding with truth in my heart to what is being said? If your answer is yes, stick to it and abandon the rest.

Courage to ride through criticism is a very useful quality to have. Oprah Winfrey once said: "Every single bit of pain I have experienced in my life was a result of me worrying about what another person was thinking of me". How much time and energy do you waste trying to get external validation? How different would your life be if you could let go of that need?

Make peace with the reality that it is impossible to please everyone. Here is your new motto: "What other people think of me is none of my business." Repeat this statement to yourself often. Are you trying to control things that are *outside* of your control? Like how other people react, or what they think of you? Resolve today that you will let go of all stress about things you cannot control. Focus your energy on the things you can influence.

The martial art Aikido teaches us about being strong without ever harming someone who is in conflict with us. It has been defined as a 'way of blending energy'.

I wonder what it would be like to experiment with forgiveness at work? How would you begin? Well, maybe simply by reflecting on those workplace situations that annoy or grieve you, or in which you have been mistreated or wronged. We create rules in our head for how people should behave. Resenting people for ignoring our rules is crazy. We can't punish anyone by refusing to forgive them.

Try letting yourself feel the feelings associated with those experiences - but without acting on them. Sometimes wisdom emerges from such reflecting and a way towards forgiveness and useful action emerges just by your making room for the feelings and waiting quietly beside them. Often any attack on you is about them and not you. Realise that people come from the limit of their own growth and experience – do not allow them to press your 'hot buttons'. Keep moving forward in your mind to the next positive episode in your life.

Break it down into easy steps. The first step is to stop saying or doing unkind things even if you feel you have been wronged. The truth is you are probably nursing your hurt: rehearsing it in your imagination, talking to others about it, plotting fantasy revenge…you know the routine. You can't change the actions of that person, but you can change your own.

Step two is to let go of the anger and try to forgive. Some people find strength by praying for the other person. Others hold onto the issue and keep it alive and suffer. If you can move forward without incriminations, things will change – there will be a shift in attitude somewhere along the line – and sooner than you think.

It reminds me of the wry wisdom in my mother's words: "Failing to forgive another person is like taking poison and expecting that other person to die" Take a look at the poisons you take at work – and, maybe, even choose to stop taking them! Then breathe a deep sigh of relief! You are free. When you let go of things, they let go of you.

OBSTACLE 1

"I have toxic colleagues!"

Any time people come together there will be personal differences. You don't usually choose the people you work with, so extra effort is often required to keep the office harmonious. When people are faced with a hostile work environment, they tend to forget the things they did to start or keep the ball rolling. Take home message: What we think, say and do has consequences. Too often we act as if we were unfamiliar with that kind of responsibility in the workplace.

You can't completely dissolve all friction in the office, but you can dissolve your stress at being caught up in the tension. As with everything in life it is not the situations you are faced with so much as your *reaction* to them that will determine your experience. Instead of getting drawn into the situation and getting angry, take a deep breath and focus instead on how lucky you are to be breathing. Try it! It diffuses the situation immediately and puts things into perspective.

When we learn respect for our peers, we can come to accept their differences. We can learn to use those differences for our mutual benefit. Along with respect comes acceptance of the inherent right of each person to follow their chosen life path, and also that diversity and variety lead to a rich mixture of humanity. Without respect we have only conflict and hostility.

Think of it as a partnership. Encourage a balanced and fair way of being and working together. Use honest disagreement rather than hostility as a way forward. The attempt by us to achieve total self sufficiency and independence emerges from the illusory separateness of the ego. As we participate in economic life we learn that we are part of an interdependent web of complex interactions and changes in one part of the web affect all of us involved. Establishing just, harmonious and honest relationships is the key to economic well-being for all.

CASE STUDY

Benjamin worked for the brokerage arm of a large investment bank. When he came to see me, he'd been there three months. His problem was that he could not stand his colleagues! Gossip was the currency in this office; it was what people exchanged as a token of friendship. But it was far from friendly to whoever's back happened to be turned at the time. Benjamin knew that he, too, was getting this treatment once out of earshot and it made him uneasy.

More worrying to him, he had, out of desire for approval, allowed himself to be pulled into this cruel sport and become one of the office's most vicious satirists. He was now anxious to stop. Problem was, he had fallen into a pattern of talking in this way with certain colleagues. How would he break that pattern?

The first thing we established is that the only person he had control over was himself. However, he needed to realise that the control he had was complete and existed for a reason. I asked him what sort of person he wanted to be in the office. He told me he wanted to be someone who acted with integrity. He decided that from now on every word he uttered about another person would be in line with how he'd like others to speak about him. And I reminded him that if he treated others this way, it wouldn't be long before that was the very treatment he himself was getting back.

So we prepared what he would say and how he would act next time one of his colleagues approached him at the water fountain fishing for gossip. He had various ways of handling this, depending on how the conversation panned out. He would start by simply sticking to saying only positive things; in many instances this would be sufficient. However, if he was pushed he could make his position clear; state firmly that he had decided not to speak negatively anymore.

Benjamin did just this and the results were astonishing to him. He found that when he did not feed the gossip others put in front of him, it soon died. Also, by raising his own standards, he had created a new way of interacting for others to flow into. On the whole, the colleagues to whom Benjamin explained his change in behaviour reacted by saying how pleased they were, as they had been unhappy with the negative mood in the office too. Not everyone felt the same, of course. Those who could not give up the gossip habit carried on as before. But over time they were in a minority.

REFLECT

Ask yourself: Do you take 100% responsibility for your life? If you don't, you are waiting for something outside of you to make your life better.

If you don't like the responses you are getting from others, the first thing you'll need to change is *your* responses to *them.*

OBSTACLE 2

"My boss makes my life hell!"

One of the complaints I hear most often is about difficult bosses. This problem goes all the way back to caveman times, I'm sure! Of course, one option is finding a new job, but there is no guarantee the new boss will be any better. The people in our life are our teachers. It doesn't mean you have to like them. If your boss makes you angry, then this is your opportunity to learn to deal with your anger effectively. You have a practice buddy! Continually ask yourself: 'What am I learning from this?'

Every experience we go through is a mirror. If we are unhappy, the experience provides us with an opportunity to change our thoughts, create new energies and respond differently. Start looking closely at what goes on between your ears. Change that and you can change your life. It's a choice you make. This determines our place in the world.

People who have problems with their bosses, especially if this problem tends to follow them from job to job, often have unresolved issues around authority. It indicates an emotional charge attached to authority, and may also point to unresolved business with parents which may need attention.

Just because your boss criticises you it doesn't mean he is right and you should start to panic about your job security. Your boss needs you too. Don't take it personally; it's just the pecking order. Don't get into the vicious circle of taking it out on those over whom you have authority. Do your work to the best of your abilities and take the high road of refusing to get caught up in it.

Make him look good in front of others. Actively listen to his concerns. He will find greater trust in you and this will be the start of a mutually comfortable relationship in the office. Notice how the energy around you both becomes lighter and free-flowing. He will be more willing to accept your ideas.

If the only problem is the person you report to, think about all other aspects of the job before deciding whether to pack it in. Can you rise above this? Develop your inner resources to help cultivate a thicker skin? Ask yourself: "What can I learn from this?" The Tao teaches that no one can hurt you when you have found your highest path.

CASE STUDY

Sally was a marketing manager in her late twenties who came to me because her boss's grand-standing actions at her expense made her feel invisible. He fronted all of her work and she got no recognition for it, though she did get a huge salary. When she came to see me she was frustrated, angry, and busy fantasising about resigning. However, everything else about the job was great so this was a drastic step. The first thing she had to get clear about was that she was unfulfilled due to her own attachment to getting the recognition she thought she deserved. Fulfilment must come from within. She couldn't see the tremendous brilliance of what she already achieved and did.

Because her boss did not value her she allowed this to affect her and make her incapable of valuing herself. It was his problem; he didn't show her appreciation. She realised that although she played a role in his success, she was not irreplaceable. Be realistic! Remember the thousand of eager graduate trainees dying for your job! She wanted to keep hers so I suggested she keeps a non-attachment to her perceived 'profile' in her company and find her personal value in a job well done. She missed one major point: You don't work for your boss. You work for yourself. None of your employers or colleagues is going to be perfect, but your job is to give your best.

In this case, as in many, it was a simple situation of two individuals not seeing eye to eye; two people with different strengths and limitations in the way they communicate. Although you cannot change your boss's management style, you can adapt your response to him. Experts call this 'managing up' as opposed to just expecting to be managed. You could be kinder about the flaws in your boss's approach and try to be more supportive towards him even if your values are polarised.

REFLECT

Buddhist philosophy asserts that outward conflicts between people are almost always a product of inner conflicts within those people. Message: resolve your internal conflict about prestige and recognition and recapture your original enthusiasm for your work.

OBSTACLE 3

"The corporate culture at my firm is all wrong"

We have seen in earlier chapter the types of attitudes and issues in the workplace that put employees off and an arrogant, bullying leader is one of the worst scenarios. Business leaders have a choice: they can build bridges or create barriers with their staff. Talking down to them will just create tension and cause resentment to build up. A healthy company needs empowered and benevolent workers and leaders. This ripples into happy customers and greater profits.

CASE STUDY

Fiona worked for a small publishing company. It was run by a man staff referred to behind his back as 'the dinosaur'. This chairman had started the company himself 25 years ago and though it was still successful, it was nowhere near its potential. Everyone, but 'the dinosaur' could see it. This was because this man was set in his ways and would not allow the many talented people beneath him to shine. Over the years this attitude had permeated its way down through the company into a culture of bosses caring more about their own entrenched positions than helping their staff develop.

No one below board level had any authority; the tiniest things had to be signed off by the powers that be. Fiona was a junior business manager in charge of a group of specialist magazines. She had been at the company only a year and was getting increasingly disillusioned. She thought she had done her research properly before joining the company, but it hadn't included talking to anyone who actually worked there. At her previous firm, Fiona had enjoyed a great deal of autonomy and the freedom to develop projects of her choice and bring them to fruition. Here, her creativity was completely stymied.

Fiona was incredibly frustrated when she came to see me, but we quickly worked out that her situation was very simple. She would have no trouble finding a position more in line with her expectations at a different company. Her level of dissatisfaction meant that unless things changed in her present company, that was the best option. She talked this over with her immediate superior, who felt just as she did about 'the dinosaur'. He made an appointment to see this man and outline some of their ideas for making their department more efficient. The result was that this man was told off for speaking out of turn and shouted out of the chairman's office.

Fiona now wrote a letter to this chairman, telling him that she sadly felt her position to be untenable. However, she left the door open for negotiations should he wish to go down this road. He didn't. She was called by the human resources department the same day and told that she should leave immediately. Although she'd be paid for her notice period, they did not wish her to work it. Fiona quickly found a better position at a progressive company and does not regret her decision to take charge of her fate. Sadly, not every company is going to become a great place to work. The trick is in recognising what you can change and what you cannot. You can change your attitude or change your job. You can't change the ogre.

REFLECT

The spiritual forum is a valuable commodity – and it's free! They are popping up in more and more forward-thinking companies. They are not about universal agreement on everything, but about a meeting of different mindsets. It's good to listen to others talking about the spiritual issues that affect them. Who could you approach in your company to suggest this idea?

CHAPTER TWELVE

The Breakthrough

"You can't solve a problem on the same level that created it"

Albert Einstein

Renewal and regeneration happen every day. Each day is new, a chance to change our life if we wish. Each moment is a chance to do something differently. In his seminars, motivational speaker Tony Robbins often reminds audiences that once they make the decision, they can transform their lives 'in a heartbeat'.

Now that you have read through the previous few pages, are you any clearer about where you need to go from here? In a nutshell, your decisions will fall into one of two broad categories. It's more likely than not that you will be able to transform your experience within your current job. However, some of you, while reading this book, will have felt a growing sense that you need to leave your current job, company or profession. And I know from experience that quite a few of you are now just plain confused; uncertain about what you should do with this knowledge.

Once again, the path to peace is the following: *change what you can't accept then accept what you can't change*. To do otherwise is to leave yourself in a state of frustration and resentment which will prevent you from being your best. To stay clear and fresh, rivers must keep moving. So must you. Serious introspection and profound change can come without a whiff of crisis. That is wisdom at its best. After all, there is nothing in the definition of change that necessitates disharmony. Think of this as an opportunity for personal growth and for fine tuning aspects of your life that you may have neglected to your detriment. Different periods of life focus one's energy differently.

Is it logical to stay in a job you hate? Probably not. There are no medals for spending a lifetime doing something you hate. But that doesn't mean there is an *immediate* answer to the next question: "What am I supposed to do now then?" It is easy to fall prey to fear of the unknown. Perhaps what you are supposed to be doing just now is *not knowing* what you are meant to be doing just now. Step away from the egotism of presuming that you should know. Turning down a road with no map can be anxiety-producing and exhilarating at the same time. Our footing is less certain, but look at the expanded views.

If you are confused about what you love doing, maybe you stopped listening to yourself a long time ago. Try this: let go of doing habitual things for a day or two – away from your routine. You will start to see things more clearly and notice what you are noticing. Next time a little voice says 'This is exciting' LISTEN. Go to the library and notice what grabs you on the shelves. Try new things. Give yourself some time and space to be by yourself. You are not likely to find your life direction while slumped in front of the television.

See an undefined future as an opportunity rather than a problem. Think: "I'm so lucky to be entering a phase of my life in which I don't need answers." When we put aside reasoning, we make some of our greatest discoveries. Electricity was not discovered using reasoning, and neither were polio vaccines. Just start experimenting. There's no reason to let the arbitrary 'barriers' of age or stage of life stop you from doing whatever is in your heart. I know a woman who graduated at age 82.

Have you noticed how we seek security, but as soon as we have it we risk it. Watch a toddler look around to check his mother is there, and then venture further away. It is the promise of new discoveries that drives us. We try to balance our lives between the comfort of security and the excitement of new experiences.

Shifting is a gradual and continuous process and that never stops. You have to be continually devoted through whatever practice works for you. Remember also, that doing what you love is not a sure fire guarantee for an easier life. It is a recipe for a fulfilling, meaningful life where you are likely to embrace more responsibilities.

We create our limitations, we must destroy them. We say things like " I can't reach that dream, I need money to start that business" or "What's the point, I am only ever going to be an Accountant because this job pays the bills" We often love our issues, our problems and want to keep them. They form our identity – what would we be without our problems eh? What would you do with your life if you had no problems? Please think deeply about this. If you look carefully at the structure of your mind, you will see that you take great meaning from solving your problems. But instead of solving them and being grateful we must create another problem! If it is not real, you will create one or go out and borrow someone else's! I would challenge you to try living the next month believing you had no problems. Watch your resistance.

CHAPTER THIRTEEN

A Richer Life

"We make a living by what we get, but we make a life by what we give."

Winston Churchill

Alice: Would you tell me, please, which way I ought to go from here?
Cat: That depends a good deal on where you want to get to.
Alice: I don't much care where.
Cat: Then it doesn't matter which way you go.

From 'Alice in Wonderland' by Lewis Carroll

"The cost of a thing is the amount of life which is required to be exchanged for it, immediately or in the long run."

Henry David Thoreau

As you lie in your bed at night, what tugs at your heartstrings? Opportunity knocks not only once, but constantly until we answer the call. Often we ignore it or are afraid to answer. The choice is yours.

Only when you become tired of needless suffering will you take the steps to move beyond it. Have you had enough yet? Why wait for the next nervous breakdown, redundancy, divorce or heart attack to change the situation?

One of the most striking insights I have had is that when we spend our time doing things like worrying, arguing our points, procrastinating or mindless consumption – we are giving away our LIFE ENERGY which we have a limited supply of. Ask yourself the next time you feel fear or anxiety brewing up inside – is this worth x hours of my life energy? Your view of your life will change. Get rid of phrases like 'I should', 'I ought' and 'there was no choice' from you vernacular. Guilt has no place in the power of personal choice. These thoughts create unnecessary pressure.

The simpler life with deeper meaning, more time for loved ones, less attachment to status symbols is not for everyone, but its appeal is growing because it improves quality of life. Why? Because it is in line with natural principles. You don't have to lower your standard of living. You will find you have enormous vitality because your time is spent working at things you enjoy and because you have created an environment you are best suited to. You won't get bored or tired because there is harmony in your character and your choice of work.

Imagine getting up in the morning and looking forward to the day ahead. A less cluttered, less consumer-driven life will help you thrive on this path to freedom and financial independence. Don't fall into the trap of believing your self worth and psychological security comes from your job title and what you earn. That is society's conditioning and you don't need to swallow the bait. Our belief that 'more is better' is not fulfilling. When you are taking your last few breaths will you really be thinking of the properties you did or did not buy at the right time? My work with hospice cancer patients certainly puts it all into context. The biggest regrets that they share with me are not doing things that they really wanted to do and not spending enough time with the people that really matter.

If we want to enjoy work environments that support and sustain life, we must begin by recognising that where life resides is in the heart. You are at the perfect place to use your head and heart to elevate yourself and your business. The very fact that you have chosen to read this book is a sign that you are ready for new possibilities that can change your experience of the workplace forever.

A life of purpose is built step by step. Start your journey. Set small goals and go for them. They will immediately make you feel better. Once you have decided, make a commitment to stick to your decision. This will only happen if you develop the habit of personal integrity and this is simply keeping your personal promises.

Your awakening is a gradual shift and you might notice the trademarks of a corporate head and spiritual heart manifesting in your life: a spontaneous generosity of spirit, a willingness to embrace spiritual principles in your work, and a transformation whereby you are no longer driven by fear and acquisition. It will seem natural and easier to access flow while remaining fully engaged in all the events unfolding around you.

Glow from the inside, play vigorously to taste the joy of living that is your birthright – but don't play only to win. Do not underestimate what you do when you work and play. Your mindset is very significant and contributes not only to your well-being but to our amazing world.

Even what you do in the next minute and the spirit in which you do it can make a huge difference. Our richness lies in the lives we have touched and the way in which we make a difference during our time on this planet. As Mahatma Gandhi wisely advised: "Be the change you want to see in the world."

Many lives are run on default. What will be the shock or unknown event that jolts you out of automatic pilot? Give yourself the chance to reflect and to embrace those long lost dreams and aspirations by making time to consciously evaluate your strengths, habits and needs and define clearly what you want and will be happiest doing.

Randy Crawford sings that hauntingly beautiful song: "One day I'll fly away..." How can you make your 'one day' happen now?

REFERENCES

Chapter One

Page 5. Tom Peters. *In Search Of Excellence: Lessons From America's Best-Run Companies.* Harper Collins, London, 1984.

Chapter Two

Page 14. Mihaly Csikszentmihalyi, *Finding Flow,* Basic Books, 1997
Page 15. Eckhart Tolle. *The Power Of Now.* New World Library, USA, 1999.

Chapter Three

Page 20. Alain de Botton. *Status Anxiety.* Penguin, London, 2005.
Page 22. Robert Kiyosaki. *Rich Dad, Poor Dad: What The Rich Teach Their Kids About Money That The Poor And Middle Class Do Not.* Little Brown, USA, 2000.
Page 25: Global Equity Strategy, *It doesn't pay: Materialism and the pursuit of happiness.* Dresdner Kleinwort Wasserstein, 3 November 2005.
Page 26: The Foundation for Inner Peace. *A Course In Miracles.* Arkana. USA, 1997.
Page 26: Oprah Winfrey. *O, The Oprah Magazine.* September 2001 Edition.

Chapter Four

Page 30. Charles Handy. *The Age Of Paradox.* Harvard Business School Press, USA, 1995.
Page 32. Joe Tye. *Staying On Top: When The World's Upside Down.* Paradox 21 Press, USA, 1996.

Chapter Five

Page 42. Elizabeth Debold. *What Is Enlightenment* magazine. Article entitled 'The business of saving the world' in the March 2005 issue.
Page 43. Alfie Kohn. *No contest: The Case Against Competition.* Mariner Books, USA, 1992.

Chapter Six

Page 49. Richard Barrett. *Liberating the Corporate Soul.* Butterworth-Heinemann, USA, 1998.
Page 51. James C. Collins & Jerry I. Porras. *Built To Last: Successful Habits of Visionary Companies.* Harper Collins, USA, 1997.
Page 55. Manfred Kets de Vries. Article entitled *High Anxiety.* The Guardian on 17 September 2005.
Page 56. Ken Blanchard, Bill Hybels, Phil Hodges. *Leadership by the Book: Tools To Transform Your Workplace.* William Morrow, 1999, USA.

Chapter Seven

References and quotes in this chapter are taken from 'The business of saving the world' by Elizabeth Debold in the March 2005 issue of *What Is Enlightenment* magazine, unless otherwise stated.
Page 65. James C. Collins & Jerry I. Porras. *Built To Last: Successful Habits of Visionary Companies.* Harper Collins, USA, 1997.
Page 68. Joe Tye. *Staying On Top: When The World's Upside Down.* Paradox 21 Press, USA, 1996.

Chapter Ten

Page 88. Abraham Maslow first introduced the concept of his hierarchy of needs in his 1943 paper 'A Theory Of Human Motivation' published in *Psychological Review,* Issue 50.
Page 89. Eckhart Tolle. *The Power Of Now.* New World Library, USA, 1999.

Chapter Eleven

Page 100. Laura B Randolph. *Oprah opens up about her weight, her wedding and why she withheld the book – Oprah Winfrey – Cover Story.* Ebony Magazine, October 1993.

NOTES